Bonnin and Morris of Philadelphia

*An Institute book on the arts
and material culture in early America*

*The Institute of Early American History and Culture
is sponsored jointly
by The College of William and Mary in Virginia
and The Colonial Williamsburg Foundation.*

Bonnin and Morris
of
Philadelphia

THE FIRST AMERICAN
PORCELAIN FACTORY, 1770-1772

by Graham Hood

Published for
the Institute of Early American History and Culture
at Williamsburg, Virginia,
by The University of North Carolina Press
Chapel Hill

Manufactured in the United States of America
Printed by Heritage Printers, Inc., Charlotte, N.C.
ISBN 0–8078–1200–5
Library of Congress Catalog Card Number 72–81327

Contents

Foreword

———————————◆••◆—————————————

For all close students of English porcelain what may be called "the American question" has tended to nag in the background, on the periphery of their conscious interest. It had long been known that Wedgwood had obtained a consignment of clay from South Carolina; that earlier, in 1765, Caleb Lloyd in Charleston had consigned to Richard Champion in Bristol a "box of Porcelaine Earthe" for the Worcester china works; and that earlier still, in 1745, William Cookworthy himself "had lately with me, the person who has discovered the *China Earth. . . .* It was found on the back of Virginia. . . ." At a later date we were introduced to the character of Andrew Duché, who pretended to have made porcelain from the Cherokee clay. It is perhaps therefore no great cause for wonder that it should be an Englishman who should take up in real earnest the study of the early history of porcelain-making in America, and it was Mr. Hood who finally gave us a rounded account of the Duché episode. Now he has taken on the more important question of the Bonnin and Morris factory—more important because it looked to the home market, was run on a large scale, and had at least a few wares attributed to it. Its very existence only penetrated the consciousness of the outside world with the publication of E. A. Barber's *The Pottery and Porcelain of the United States of*

America in 1893. Subsequent publications in this century seemed to add little but confusion. Mr. Hood has now tackled the problem in a fundamental way, following up and expanding the documentation of the factory in records and printed sources; studying closely and analyzing the nature of the wares already attributed to the factory, and expanding this corpus of material; and finally, and decisively, arranging for excavation on the factory site and thus finally removing from the arena of doubt the exact nature of the porcelain made at the Philadelphia factory. His book is a true classic of ceramic research.

ROBERT J. CHARLESTON
Keeper of Ceramics and Glass
Victoria and Albert Museum

Preface

———————◆•◆•◆———————

This book came into being in a way I can only describe as circumambulatory. All the work it involved was fitted into and around my regular occupation; thus, its development from 1965 to 1970 was as spasmodic as my leisure hours. My interest in Bonnin and Morris was sparked by a chance remark of John Sweeney's at the Winterthur Museum and a fortuitous discovery in the storerooms of the Yale University Art Gallery. Further investigation, however, revealed only a multitude of hydra-headed problems that kept cropping up, in one way or another, with such unfailing regularity that I frequently despaired of solving them. Not until the summer of 1968 were the last and most important questions answered by an archaeological investigation of the site of the Bonnin and Morris factory. Had I been able to devote more of my professional time to all the problems, or had I been cleverer, I would have been able to tighten the sequences of, and thus shorten, the research. But that undoubtedly would have removed the element of serendipity that made the whole venture so enjoyable.

I wish to acknowledge, with particular gratitude, grants from the American Philosophical Society (Penrose Fund) and Yale University (Morse Fund), which enabled me to study related ceramics in England in the summer of 1966;

[xi]

and three grants from the Robert L. McNeil, Jr., Foundation, Inc., of Philadelphia, which contributed greatly toward the archaeological investigation of the factory site in the fall of 1967 and enabled me to organize, in the summer of 1968, all the material I had gathered. To members of the Morris family of Philadelphia, Roland Morris, Mrs. James Rawle, Mrs. William F. Machold, William Rawle, and Price Slattery, I cannot adequately convey my thanks for their willingness to support a research enterprise, which they realized was not only connected with their family long ago but was also important in the history of Philadelphia and in the development of American ceramics. These individuals contributed enormously to the realization of the archaeological work. Their aid was given in memory of James Rawle 2nd, antiquarian and historian of Philadelphia, who was vitally interested in this project but who did not live to see its outcome. Finally, a grant from The Colonial Williamsburg Foundation made the publication of the book possible. I am grateful to its president, Carlisle H. Humelsine, for his support.

This book really belongs to Bob and Nancy McNeil. They offered me a warm haven in Philadelphia, suggested many new and ingenious approaches, and, quite simply, turned dreams into realities. Their interest and involvement were admirable.

Many good souls have given me invaluable help. My wife, Gale, continually spurred my interest, prompted me to new investigations, and, with contagious enthusiasm, urged me at times of faintheartedness to continue with the work. Jules Prown encouraged me to pursue this study from the very beginning, and I owe a great debt, as in many other things, to his continuing perspicacity, friendship, and support. John Cotter became so interested in the possible archaeological resolution of the problems involved in this project that he quite gratuitously took his summer school class in archaeology from the University of Pennsylvania to the site of the factory and discovered the particular area that we were later able to excavate. This discovery really acted as the catalyst in precipitating the dig, and I am especially grateful to Dr. Cotter for his spontaneous participation. Furthermore, it was through his agencies that I met Paul R. Huey and Garry Wheeler Stone, who actually carried out the excavation. I was as impressed with the high degree of professionalism they brought to the operation as I was delighted by their enthusiasm. The last part of this book utilizes the report they made of their work. We would not have been able to dig at all had it not been for the kindness of the owner of the property, Mr. William Bell, who not only gave his permission but materially aided our progress.

During my visit to England I was fortunate in meeting Lieutenant Colonel P. D. S. Palmer, J.P., D.L., a direct descendant of Bonnin's father-in-law, who willingly shared with me the results of his researches and allowed me to copy Bonnin's letters. I also benefited greatly by conversations with Robert Charleston, John Mallet, Bernard Watney, and Hugh Tait. They shared their knowledge and experience with me then and have continued to do so since, for which I am deeply grateful. Henry Maynard first interested me in ceramics and generously taught me a great deal; he is the book's godfather.

In addition, I would like to extend special thanks to Frederick J. Cummings, Andrew C. Ritchie, Miss Mavis Bimson, the late A. J. Toppin, C.V.O., Milo Naeve, Mrs. Susan Richardson, and Willis F. Woods. Charles Cunningham, David duBon, Carl Dauterman, Jonathan Fairbanks, Miss Mary Glaze, Calvin Hathaway, Philip G. Nordell, Mrs. Susan Sack, Marvin Schwartz, Lloyd Skarsgaard, Miss Jane Sugden, and John Sweeney have also given me valuable help.

GRAHAM HOOD
The Colonial Williamsburg Foundation

Bonnin and Morris of Philadelphia

Introduction

———— ✦•✦ ————

In 1770 Gousse Bonnin and George Anthony Morris built a factory in Philadelphia for the manufacture of "American China." Apparently using clay from the banks of the Delaware River near Wilmington and employing skilled workmen especially brought from England, the partners attempted to produce soft-paste porcelain patterned on contemporary English wares. After two years of difficulties with finances, workmen, and material, the factory failed. Few of the wares have survived.

Such is the standard account of the factory; it appears in histories of Philadelphia from the early nineteenth century onward and in the histories of American ceramics beginning with E. A. Barber's monumental *Pottery and Porcelain of the United States*.[1] In view of the factory's unusual ambitions, it seems far from adequate. Moreover, the exact nature of the wares presumed to have been made by Bonnin and Morris has caused much confusion. Barber listed only one object— a fruit basket attributed to the factory by a local historian of note, Dr. James Mease, in 1841—and called it "cream-coloured ware . . . decorated in blue" (figs. 1–4). John Spargo later described it as "white earthenware" but conjectured that "some part of the wares must have been soft-paste porcelain or bone-china."[2] John Ramsey attributed three pieces of "fine white earthenware" to Bonnin and Morris (figs. 1–9) but erroneously described the underglaze mark "P" on the pieces as "a small old style 's' resembling our modern 'p' underglaze."[3] Arthur W. Clement assembled more documentary evidence of the factory than had previously appeared and included three more attributed pieces (figs. 10–15).[4] He stated that "all five pieces are white glazed earthenware and not porcelain," although four years later he examined one of these objects and announced that it was soft-paste porcelain.[5]

Not only did these scholars describe so differently the wares they attributed to Bonnin and Morris, but they also based their attribution, in the absence of archaeological evidence, on the aforementioned fruit basket, known since 1841. They accepted at face value a documentary connection between this piece and the Bonnin and Morris factory, which, when isolated and closely examined, appears highly questionable. If that object could not be proved to have been made by Bonnin and Morris, the attribution of the whole group was open to doubt.

Thus, when I began my investigation, a curious situation prevailed. The factory was long known, but very little of substance had ever been written about it; the first chapter of this book attempts to remedy that defect. And the group of wares that was discussed and so variously described by several scholars was never proven by them to have been made by Bonnin and Morris; the second chapter reveals the steps by which these anomalies were resolved.

The Bonnin and Morris factory was the only colonial factory ambitious enough to try and make porcelain on a commercial scale. Careful examination of the pertinent documentary material revealed that the factory achieved a considerable and diverse production in proportion to its size. It seemed necessary to discover if its products matched its sophisticated ambitions. If the known wares were in fact made by Bonnin and Morris and if they were porcelain rather than the earthenware that scholars had previously claimed them to be, the factory was unique—the first of its kind in America and the only one in the eighteenth century. The partners' impetus would then be construed as a colonial manifestation of the contemporary English rage for porcelain, and their initiative seen as a colonial counterpart of the estimable English porcelain factories of that time. The Bonnin and Morris factory would thus antedate the Philadelphia factory of William Ellis Tucker, always previously regarded as the pioneer in the manufacture of porcelain in America, by more than fifty years.[6]

The Factory

By 1770 Philadelphia had become, after London, one of the largest and wealthiest cities in the British Empire and was, consequently, a most promising location for a porcelain factory.[7] Its citizens had a great taste for luxuries, which inevitably included, in the third quarter of the eighteenth century, hard- and soft-paste porcelains. If superb and fashion-conscious craftsmen such as Joseph Richardson, the silversmith, and Thomas Affleck, the cabinetmaker, flourished in Philadelphia by catering to their fellow citizens' tastes, it was inevitable that someone would see in the English porcelain factories of the time a suggestion for a prosperous colonial industry. Philadelphians had long bought an enormous amount of imported delft and stoneware and by 1770 were turning eagerly to the novel Wedgwood queensware. They also had a taste for hard-paste porcelain to judge from the frequent advertisements in Philadelphia newspapers for "India China," while Bow soft-paste porcelain was imported into America at least as early as 1754.[8] In addition to this rich local market, the Nonimportation Agreement, which was specifically designed to support colonial industries during the postwar depression of the late 1760s, would seem to have created a most propitious atmosphere for the establishment of a domestic porcelain factory.

Before they entered into partnership in 1769, Gousse Bonnin and George Anthony Morris appear to have led relatively uneventful lives. Neither is known to have had any prior connection with a pottery or porcelain factory. Morris seems to have had a singularly sheltered existence. He was born between the end of 1742 and 1745 into a prominent Philadelphia family, the son of Joseph (1715-1785) and Martha Fitzwater Morris. In 1767 he was living with his father on Front Street. In the spring of 1772 he went to North Carolina, where he died on October 5, 1773; no will is recorded in North Carolina or in Philadelphia. His participation in the factory was probably limited to a financial interest, although he doubtless had many influential and useful contacts in Philadelphia through his family. He presumably managed the affairs of the factory during Bonnin's absences in England. Apart from his connection with this enterprise, nothing is known of him.[9]

Gousse Bonnin was the grandson of a Huguenot refugee of the same name, who had signed an indenture with Sir Matthias Vincent in 1686 in return for certain lands in Pennsylvania.[10] The original Gousse eventually became a surgeon in Antigua. His will was proved August 18, 1713. Henry Bonnin, his son, was born about 1688 and became a prosperous merchant in Antigua. He married in 1735 and had one daughter, Margaret, and two sons, Henry and Gousse, none of whom were baptized in Antigua. Gousse was educated at Eton College from 1754 to 1759; assuming, therefore, that he left Eton at the normal age, he was probably born about 1741. He seems to have led a life of leisure for the next six or seven years, since his name is not found in university, Inns of Court, army, or apprentice records. Confirmation of this— together with a rare insight into his personality, which appears impulsive and volatile, with opportunist overtones— may be found in a letter written to his mother-in-law when he was deeply involved in the porcelain factory (November 9, 1771): "I frequently smile at the wide diffrence, between my former and present pursuits in life, as also at the futile presages of those, who confidently foretold the impracticability, of my ever becoming a proficient in industry, and application, to business. That this is a strange world, is the repeated acknowledgement of every age, perhaps you'll say my Amendment is as strange . . . however you may rest assured, the lively sun of Gallantry and Jollity is set with me, and gives place, to the Calmer light of unremitted assiduity, in the furtherance of the China Manufactory" (Appendix 4).

Bonnin married Dorothy Palmer on October 4, 1766, in the parish church of St. Martin in the Fields, London. At the time he was about twenty-five and she was thirty-one, the sixth child of Sir Charles Palmer Bt. of Dorney, Buckinghamshire. Both Henry Bonnin and Sir Charles Palmer settled money on their children; the first by indenture (the rent of land and houses) dated August 11, 1767, the latter by a marriage settlement (of £500 paid at once and £1,500 upon his death) dated December 8, 1767. The first child of this marriage, Charles Henry Bonnin, was baptized at Burnham (adjacent to Dorney), Buckinghamshire, on August 19, 1767.

Shortly thereafter Bonnin applied to the crown for a grant of twenty thousand acres in East Florida, a large territory that was one of the spoils of the recent Seven Years' War. Impatient, perhaps, with the inevitable delay in proceedings and anxious to complete the voyage before a second child was born, Bonnin sailed for America with his family in May 1768. They arrived in Philadelphia in August.[11] Sometime within the next six or seven months, according to Henry Bonnin's letter to Sir Charles Palmer of September 21, 1770, Bonnin borrowed £600 from an unknown source. This, beyond his regular income and the capital received at his marriage, seems a good deal more than was necessary for living expenses. He may well have used part of the money to purchase specialized knowledge and assistance in a commercial venture, for in 1769 he was back in London to seek a patent for the manufacture of black lead crucibles. The patent was acknowledged July 27, 1769.[12] According to Bonnin's specification, the crucibles were to be made from "a species of clay hitherto only discovered near the city of Philadelphia" mixed with an equal quantity of prepared black lead or graphite. "Of this mixture or cement the crucibles are formed upon a potter's wheel in the same manner as glazed or other pots, and undergo the same operation of heat to harden them. It is easy to discover any flaw in the crucibles by sounding them, as is customary with china."

The patent application indicates Bonnin's developing interest in ceramics.The manufacture of both crucibles and porcelain demanded the knowledgeable preparation of particular kinds of clays and the construction of high-firing kilns. Yet it is highly unlikely that the patent application was a premeditated step toward the manufacture of porcelain. A patent for crucibles would not protect a porcelain factory, nor is there any evidence that crucibles were made or that the patent was anything but an expense to Bonnin: "This is no Country to assert the privileges of a Patent, without which the Crucibles could not be momentous, as the fabrication, when once begun, is so extremely open, and simple, as to render it impossible to be preserved a secret. If ever it is my fate to reside in Great Britain, there they will shine with proper lustre, duely supported by the Authority of the King, not so here."[13] Indeed, from the advertisement in the *Pennsylvania Chronicle* (Philadelphia), October 9, 1769 (Appendix 5), it seems that Bonnin had not at that time discovered or acquired any notable source of supply of this black lead.

Bonnin allowed himself little time to develop the crucible factory before forming a partnership with Morris for the manufacture of "American China." The first indication of this was a land agreement between himself, Morris, and the latter's sister, Phoebe, applied for December 1 and completed December 14, 1769. This concerned three-quarters of an acre of land on the west side of Front Street, about 120 feet north of Prime Street (or Wicacoa Lane, as it was generally known) in the district of Southwark; the site had good access to the river. Morris also owned an adjacent plot of land to the south and, in an agreement dated January 1 and completed September 13, 1770, rented half of it to Bonnin (fig. 18).[14]

Boldly headlined "NEW CHINA WARE," the first public announcement of the factory appeared in the *Pennsylvania Chronicle*, January 1, 1770. An appeal to the spirit of the Nonimportation Agreement is paramount: "Notwithstanding the various difficulties and disadvantages, which usually attend the introduction of any important manufacture in a new country, the proprietors of the China Works now erecting in Southwark . . . have proved to a certainty, that the clays of America are productive of as good porcelain as any heretofore manufactured at the famous factory in Bow, near London. . . ."[15] Considering that it was another year before the proprietors announced the first definite production of wares, the claim to have produced porcelain as good as Bow seems to have been an empty one indeed. And the specific citation of Bow is curious; it is the only English factory that Bonnin and Morris ever mentioned, although at that time it was several years past its prime. As no connection between the Bow factory and Bonnin and Morris has yet come to light, it can only be assumed that Bow was the porcelain best known locally, other than Chinese, to use as a standard for comparison.[16]

For the making of good porcelain, a vital necessity was a supply of excellent clay. The source of these "clays of America" that Bonnin and Morris intended to use is indicated in two documents. One, written by Dr. James Mease when he presented the aforementioned fruit basket to the Franklin Institute, describes it as *"White-Clay-Creek* in the State of Delaware, a few miles from the City of Wilmington."[17] The other, "A Memoir of Thomas Gilpin," written by the subject's son within a few years of his father's death in 1777, confirms this: "The clay ... was obtained from the banks of the Delaware between Newcastle and Wilmington and it was mixed with calcined bones."[18] There is every reason to believe that these two comments were independent reports of a single known fact, for the memoir remained in manuscript form until recently. The area was not notable at the time for containing deposits of good china-clays.[19]

In an attempt to raise capital for the factory, Bonnin returned to England immediately after forming the partnership and in February 1770 approached Sir Charles Palmer to request that the remaining £1,500 of the marriage settlement be made available to him. Sir Charles drafted, but apparently did not send, a blistering letter of refusal in which he aired his strong disapproval of the whole scheme. Subsequently, Bonnin (as related in his father's letter of September 21, 1770) borrowed £280 while in England, £200 immediately on his return to Philadelphia, and a further £520 in the following few months, for all of which his father was guarantor. In addition to his search for capital, Bonnin must have returned to England to induce skilled workmen from English porcelain factories to Philadelphia. Despite the partners' appeal in their first advertisement for "All workmen skill'd in the different branches of throw-turning, modelling, moulding and pressing, and painting," it cannot be imagined that there were any workmen in Philadelphia at that time with the specialized knowledge and experience of a porcelain factory. Bonnin and Morris even advertised for skilled workmen in the *South Carolina Gazette* (Charleston) of March 15, 1770, hoping, presumably, to entice workmen away from John

Bartlem's newly established creamware factory near Charleston, as Bartlem himself had enticed his men away from the Staffordshire factories earlier.[20]

Bonnin's visit to England produced one desired result; in October 1770 the Pennsylvania *Staatsbote* (Philadelphia) announced that "nine master workers have arrived here for the porcelain manufactory of this city." The importance of their arrival can be seen by the announcement two months later that the partners "have in some measure, answered the expectation of their friends, by their first Emission of Porcelain." This is the first indication of any kind of wares being actually produced. It is substantiated by a letter from Bonnin to Lady Palmer, dated January 15, 1771, five days after the public announcement: "I think I can now congratulate myself on the flourishing posture of our affairs, The China Factory is brought to a crisis and the first Emission of ware which took place the 24th of December was immediately bought up and most generally admired, I shall send forth another large quantity in ten days, which is already bespoke, nevertheless you may believe there are some faults in it, since no work was ever immediately brought to perfection" (Appendix 3). This letter also enclosed a bill of exchange to Sir Charles for £100, as one-third repayment of a loan from him the previous month. Sir Charles's reluctance to support the venture had probably been overcome by Henry Bonnin's persuasive letter of September 21, 1770.[21]

Bonnin and Morris advertised the "capital works of the Factory" as "compleated, and in motion" in July 1770. These appear, from descriptions of the factory incorporated in the later sales notices, to have been fairly extensive: "three kilns, two furnaces, two mills, two clay vaults, cisterns, engines, and treading room." The buildings were situated on a lot north of a new street built by the partners and called China Street (only recently changed to Alter Street) between Front and

Second streets—the site of the present Washington Avenue. South of China Street and fronting on Prime Street (now Ellsworth Street), the partners built a three-story frame building, eighty feet by fifteen feet, in which, according to the sale notice of October 19, 1774, "the principal branches of the China manufactory were carried on." This building is clearly visible on the John Hills map of Philadelphia of 1796 (fig. 16). Although the advertisement of July 1770 had stated that the factory was "in motion," Bonnin and Morris obviously depended on the English master workers for the actual production of porcelain, since there is no intimation of wares being made before January 1771. However, the partners' intentions are clearly shown by their advertised request of July 1770 for shank or knuckle bones. They intended to make soft-paste porcelain, using bone ash to fuse it, directly in the Bow tradition.[22]

Unfortunately, the names of these influential master workers are unknown, with one exception. In his previously mentioned *Address to the Workmen*, Josiah Wedgwood excoriated Bonnin and Morris after he had blasted Bartlem: "Another [china factory] equally fruitless, and equally fatal to our people (for *they* were chiefly employed in it) was carried on in Pennsylvania. Here a sort of China Ware was aimed at, and eight men went over at first; whether any more, or how many, might follow, I have not learnt. The event was nearly the same in this as in the others; the proprietors, soon finding that they had no chance of succeeding, not only gave up the undertaking, but silenced the just complaints of the poor injured workmen, by clapping one of them (Thomas Gale) into a prison; the rest who had never received half the wages agreed for, were left entirely to shift for themselves" (Appendix 12).[23]

To attract the master workers to Philadelphia, Bonnin and Morris offered twice the wages Wedgwood paid, according to the latter's *Address to the Workmen*. Details of the arrangements between proprietors and workmen can be found in the letter written later to the *Pennsylvania Chronicle*, November 14, 1772, by Wedgwood's nephew, Thomas Byerley; they include the workmen's passage to America and a weekly salary of a guinea and a half for a twelve-hour day (Appendix 9). Although all the master workmen arrived on a ship from London, it is not known if they were all English. Among the effects of the factory that Bonnin advertised for sale in May 1773 was a young German, "completely skilled" in the process of making porcelain. It was Bonnin himself, in all probability, who was described by the author of the previously quoted "Memoir of Thomas Gilpin" as "a Swiss or French Artist." What is certain is that the group of Bonnin and Morris wares is extremely close to English soft-paste porcelain and not remotely like French.[24]

Once the initial production had been achieved, Bonnin and Morris made a determined effort to speed things up "notwithstanding the designed importation of China ware by a few."[25] They engaged an independent merchant, Archibald McElroy, to expedite sales, and even at this early stage offered "compleat sets for the dining and tea table together, or dining singly." These sets included such items as picklestands, fruit baskets, sauceboats in two sizes, pint bowls, and plates.[26] Bonnin's letter to Lady Palmer indicated that the first batch was immediately sold and that the second batch, produced in January 1771, was spoken for. The next batch publicly announced on March 14, included four- and six-quart bowls. Such large bowls were difficult to fire successfully, and their appearance indicates an unexpected technical proficiency in the new enterprise. By May 1771, according to Thomas Wharton's bill (Appendix 7), the available range of objects also included plain cups, handled cups, quilted cups, sugar dishes in two sizes, cream ewers, and teapots in two sizes.

Orders seem to have been fairly numerous and came from as far away as Albany—although they were not always promptly filled. Sir William Johnson's agent in Philadelphia, Carpenter Wharton, wrote to him in Albany on October 14: "Show'd long since have done my Self the honour of Writing to you, had I not been frequently disappointed by the Managers of the China Factory in the receiving a breakfast Set a China of the Manufactory of this City (Which I beg leave to Present You for the use of the Hall,) as I flatter my Self it is the very best of the Kind they have yet exhibited. . . . I am Senceable it would afford you a Peculiar Satisfaction in observing the progress made in the China and Glass Manufactories, the demand for them is So Great, that the proprietors of the Manufactories are not able to Supply the orders from the different Colonies." Tempting as it is to see in Wharton's remarks a remarkably widespread interest in the factory, it is possible that he simply retailed the excuses he received from the partners, which are certainly reminiscent of Bonnin's magniloquent style. They have an air of the perpetual salesman's excuse for nondelivery.[27]

The partners presumably intended to decorate their wares with underglaze blue, as their advertised request for "Zaffera" in January 1771 would indicate. Fine decoration was a necessary adjunct to their wares if they were to provide any real competition with the brilliantly colored delft, polychromed Chinese export porcelain, Staffordshire stoneware, and English blue and white, all imported from England. Although "Blue and White Ware, either useful or ornamental," was not mentioned until July 1771, it may have been available from the beginning, according to a letter from Joseph Shippen, Jr., to his father, dated Philadelphia, March 15, 1771: "There have been no China Cups and Saucers made at the Factory since my last, like those which Mrs. Penn bought (tho' great quantities of an inferior kind have been made)...."[28]

Within two months of the first blue and white ware being produced Bonnin and Morris advertised in September 1771: "There will shortly be an emission from this manufactory, an assortment of both useful and ornamental Enamelled China." Not until the following January, however, did they announce that enameled porcelain was actually available: "Complete sets of Dressing Boxes for the Toilet, either in Blue or Enamel." This represented an ambitious and sophisticated addition to the factory's regular production. Unfortunately, no complete pieces are known to have survived.

Toward the end of 1771 Bonnin and Morris became acutely aware of the financial hazards of a porcelain factory, despite an apparently substantial capital investment from Bonnin's father. Labor was as short as bones were plentiful.[29] In addition, the repeal of English duties caused many Philadelphians to wonder if their rejection of English imports for the sake of local pride and industry was not too great a sacrifice. Bonnin and Morris, "actuated as strongly by the sincerest Attachment to the Interest of the Public as to our private Emolument," appealed to the Pennsylvania legislature for a loan. They submitted a sample of the kind of work they had brought into "no contemptable Train of Perfection," but the application was refused (Appendix 6). As a substitute the proprietors organized a lottery to help recoup their finances (fig. 17).[30]

Faced with the refusal of a loan from the legislature, the disintegration of the Nonimportation Agreement, the large amounts of porcelain coming into the country through the East India Company and private importers, and the "malevolent attempts of those who think it their interest to depreciate the quality of American China," Bonnin and Morris published a broadside in the *Pennsylvania Gazette* (Philadelphia), August 1, 1771, as a means of reviving interest in their wares.[31] Resorting to a rousing, hortatory epistle in support of native industries, the authors of the broadside waved the flag and beat every available drum: "The Manufacture of China Ware in this Province, certainly deserves the serious Attention of every Man, who prays for the Happiness of his Fellow-subjects, or that the very Semblance of Liberty may be handed down to Posterity. . . ." Again the factory was equated, in its ambitions and accomplishments, with Stiegel's Manheim glass factory as a compliment to colonial enterprise and virtue. But the real fear of insurmountable competition from established importers, such as the East India Company, showed through the bravado only too clearly. The authors of the broadside begged for a certain tolerance in terms of the quality and cost of the native wares, as well as a grace period of "a few Years" to refine the wares, otherwise "the Factories, Labourers and all" would "be swallowed up in the Vortex of an *East-India* Company." Much more serious than sentiment was the raw fact: "Every Importer of China knows, and most retail Purchasers have observed with Pleasure, that the Price of China is fallen Five Shillings in the Pound, since the Commencement of a China Factory in this place." It is interesting to note that it was precisely such complaints of prospective price cutting by the East India Company (with governmental abetting in the form of the Tea Act) that led to the Boston Tea Party later. In other words, protests against mercantile monopoly and political tyranny were closely interwoven, and it is probable that the sad fates of the porcelain and glass factories were not forgotten in the heat of the later conflicts.[32]

Bonnin and Morris concluded their broadside with an effort to turn economic disadvantage into a patriotic plea, proclaiming that "no less than Fifteen Thousand Pounds Worth of

China has been imported into this Province since the first of *April* last; if this Clay be paid for, there are Fifteen Thousand Pounds of Gold and Silver less in the Province than we should have had, if the same Ware had not been imported, but manufactured amongst us. . . . No Man of common Sense will venture to say, that the Province can long endure such enormous Taxes" (Appendix 8).

In the midst of so much uncertainty Bonnin was still able to offer his parents-in-law the following sanguine comments in a letter of November 9: "The business of China making . . . is a work of Critical nicety, and most extensive advantage, if rightly managed and understood. . . . I have the highest expectation of its being great in the extreme; people cease to stigmatize me for madness and folly in the undertaking; those who profess themselves my friends, applaud my *sagacious* perseverance; others with envy, cannot conceal their distracted astonishment" (Appendix 4).

Production appears to have continued until at least September 1772, despite Morris's absence in North Carolina from April onward. During that time Bonnin advertised repeatedly for painters, trained or apprentice. He may also have begun experiments with a hard-paste body; the *Pennsylvania Packet* (Philadelphia), August 3, 1772, included the Philadelphia news "that the Proprietors of the China Manufactory in this city, have lately made experiments with some clay presented to them by a Gentleman of Charlestown, South-Carolina, which produces China superior to any brought from the East-Indies, and will stand the heat beyond any kind of crucibles ever yet made." This could have been prompted by a recognition of some measure of truth behind criticisms of the quality of the wares. By November the writing was on the wall. The workmen rebelled against their working conditions—fractiousness being a not uncommon quality among potters in the eighteenth century—and sought charity openly on the streets.

Bonnin attempted to defend the proprietors' reputation, but with little conviction. In his later *Address to the Workmen* Wedgwood gave (presumably exaggerated) details with apposite relish: "Some [of the workmen] died immediately, of sickness occasioned by this great change in their prospects and manner of living, being dashed at once from the highest expectations to the lowest and most abject misery. . . . A subscription was set on foot by the inhabitants for their relief, by which those who had weathered the first storm were supplied with daily bread; but, like plants removed into a soil unnatural to them, they dwindled away and died, and not one was left alive, to return to give us any farther particulars of this affecting tale" (Appendix 12).

Wedgwood's nephew, Byerley, was in Philadelphia at this time and, according to his uncle, tried to help the disaffected workmen. An unsigned letter, apparently by Byerley (if so, he possessed his uncle's overblown literary style) appeared in the *Pennsylvania Journal* (November 11, 1772) on their behalf: "The Proprietors . . . exacted a full obedience from the men . . . but they have not so scrupulously fulfilled their own engagement . . . yet [the workmen] have not, as the advertiser would insinuate, meanly gone begging about . . . but modestly wish and desire only . . . to be restored to their own [country]. . . . The Proprietors . . . have not, as is the case of these poor people, lost their *All* . . ." (Appendix 9).

Byerley referred to "the late China Manufactory" five days before the announcement in the *Pennsylvania Chronicle* (November 14, 1772) that "the Acting Proprietor" was "under a necessity of embarking with his family for England, on board one of the first Spring ships." Bonnin was anxious to sell the factory and various lots of ground as speedily as possible. This was no easy matter, however, for they were still for sale two years later (Appendixes 10–11). Bonnin seems to have returned to England about September 1773, where he lived first in Bristol, then in a fashionable street in Worcester. He later owned race horses. Byerley's statement that the "Proprietors . . . have not . . . lost their *All*" may have been justified.[33] It is possible that Bonnin decided to close down the factory rather than risk bankruptcy. The last advertisement for the property in Philadelphia newspapers was dated October 19, 1774. Thereafter the buildings presumably began their descent into the limbo of a "sailor's brothel and riot house on a large scale" (fig. 19).[34]

The reasons for the failure of the porcelain factory are not far to seek. Bonnin persistently complained that the frequent importations of porcelain would flood the market, and merchants' advertisements in Philadelphia newspapers of the period amply confirm his gloomy prognostications. Imported wares were ever desirable, particularly when "the Price of China is fallen Five Shillings in the Pound, since the Commencement of a China Factory in this place." It was impossible to compete with the huge wholesalers in such circumstances. Bonnin was surely aware, also, that the hard-paste Chinese export porcelain could withstand any amount of boiling without cracking or discoloration and, with normal wear and tear, was a great deal more serviceable than soft-paste porcelain.[35] Quantities of this, as well as English blue and white, were shipped in, while there was a growing fashion for Wedgwood's fine and durable stoneware. In 1765 Wedgwood had been deeply concerned about possible American competition from Bartlem: "The bulk of our particular manufactures are, you know, exported to foreign markets . . . and the principal of these markets are the Continent and Islands of North America. To the Continent we send an amazeing quantity of white stoneware . . . This trade to our Colonies we are apprehensive of loseing in a few years as they have set on foot some Pot works there already."[36] But by 1770 Wedgwood seemed so confident of his own superiority that he appears never to have mentioned the Bonnin and Morris factory in his correspondence. In any case, the taste of the time was changing toward creamware, or queensware: "The demand for the said Cream color alias Queens Ware . . . still increases. It is really amazeing how rapidly the use has spread almost over the whole globe and how universally it is liked. . . . I had with me yesterday an East Indian Captain, and another Gentleman and Lady from those parts who . . . told me it was already in use there, and in much higher estimation than the present Porcellain." In 1769 Wedgwood reported that the Quakers were interested in his wares and had ordered a substantial amount. As a further indication of changing taste, in that year George Washington, who was not otherwise notable for his assiduous attention to fashion, ordered through his London agent a large consignment of "the most fashionable kind of Queens Ware."[37]

Bonnin and Morris can never have achieved a substantial enough production to compete effectively with the mass-produced Chinese porcelain or with Wedgwood. Even English blue and white appears to have been cheaper. A comparison of Bonnin and Morris prices, from the Thomas Wharton bill mentioned above, and the prices of Worcester blue and white, wholesale in England about ten years earlier, is revealing. A Bonnin and Morris teapot cost seven shillings and sixpence, while a Worcester teapot varied between one shilling and threepence and two shillings and sixpence, according to size. Bonnin and Morris cups varied between one and three shillings; Worcester cups cost threepence halfpenny each. Bonnin and Morris sauceboats ranged from one shilling to three shillings and ninepence depending on size, whereas a more elaborate Worcester two-handled sauceboat cost between two shillings and two shillings and fourpence. Plain Wedgwood queensware sauceboats, wholesale in England in 1774, cost fivepence, and a "sauce terrine" cost only two shillings. Bonnin and Morris plates, of an unspecified size, were one shilling each, while queensware plates, about ten inches in diameter, were two shillings and sixpence a dozen. An important factor in the high prices was undoubtedly the high cost of labor; it was this point that was most stressed by later commentators.[38]

The flood of imported ceramics, which poured in after the collapse of the Nonimportation Agreement, and labor difficulties must surely have convinced Bonnin of the hopelessness of his task. As no bankruptcy charges are known to have been filed against him, he was presumably prescient enough to close the factory before losing everything.

The Wares

———◆•◆———

While the documentary information of the previous chapter increases our knowledge of the factory's activities, it does not solve two crucial questions—are the objects attributed by earlier scholars to the Bonnin and Morris factory porcelain or earthenware, and, indeed, are they by Bonnin and Morris? Scientific research produced an answer to the first question— the pieces proved to be soft-paste, bone-ash porcelain. But neither scientific, historical, nor stylistic examinations could conclusively separate them from contemporary English blue and white porcelains. After those avenues of research had been exhausted it became obvious that only an archaeological investigation of the site of the factory could provide enough evidence to judge the validity of the attributed group. This chapter contains a detailed account of the various steps by which this previously known group of objects, together with several more that came to light during the investigation, was proved to have been made by Bonnin and Morris.

At first it seemed possible that a scientific examination of the wares might provide the answers to questions of both classification and origin. Bonnin and Morris claimed to have made porcelain; but eighteenth-century terminology in such matters was often imprecise, and such a claim is not indu-

bitable proof of success. All the recent authorities had classi-
fied the group of wares as some kind of earthenware—a
decision that appears to have been based on the fact that the
pieces were not translucent. To this author such a classification seemed highly questionable. The objects had all the
appearance of soft-paste porcelain to the naked eye, and,
moreover, most were dimly translucent with a strong in-
candescent light. Spot tests for the presence of phosphate in
these objects subsequently proved positive.[39] As Bonnin and
Morris frequently advertised for bones (which they presumably calcined and added to the clay) the presence of phosphate
was to be expected. And as there was no known reason for
the partners to add bone ash to a clay body for the production
of earthenware, stoneware, or creamware, one assumed that
they were consciously striving for the production of porcelain. The fact that a porcelain-type body is not translucent
does not make it any the less porcelain; much late Bow, for
example, was poorly fired and is not translucent, but is, nevertheless, soft-paste porcelain. Taking advantage of a generous
offer from the British Museum laboratory, and with the kind
cooperation of the authorities of the Philadelphia Museum of
Art, the author sent a sample of the broken fruit basket (fig.
1), and also a sample of a putative Bonnin and Morris piece
that will be discussed later (figs. 20–21), to London for quan-
titative spectrographic analysis. The result of this was that
the samples were unquestionably bone-ash porcelain.[40]

Satisfying though this solution was, it only increased the
complexities of the related problem. For the spectrographic
analysis proved that the samples contained ingredients (14–
18 percent phosphorus pentoxide, 19–23 percent calcium
oxide, and less than 1 percent lead oxide and magnesium
oxide) in quantities common to several English porcelain
factories, such as Bow, Lowestoft, Gold Anchor Chelsea,
late Derby, and Liverpool. Obviously, therefore, it was im-

possible to deduce that the samples were definitely not from any of those factories.

The historical documentation of the wares was similarly opaque. Only one piece had any documentary connection with the Bonnin and Morris factory—the broken fruit basket (fig. 1) given to the Franklin Institute in Philadelphia in 1841 by Dr. James Mease. Because this was a crucial piece the documentation, written by Dr. Mease, was carefully scrutinized:

The broken China fruit basket which I have the pleasure to present to the Franklin Institute, was part of a dinner set and the first attempt at the manufacture of china in the United States, the history of which is as follows:

Mr. Gousey Bonnin of Antigua, came to Philadelphia before the American War, and his father having been a correspondent of my father's, they became intimate. What lead him to the speculation, I never heard, but in an unfortunate hour, he resolved to undertake the manufacture of China the clay for which he procured from *White-Clay-Creek* in the State of Delaware, a few miles from the City of Wilmington, and with the aid of five hundred pounds loaned him by my father he erected a long frame building in Prime Street southward [Southwark?], which I believe now leads from the navy yard west. The workmen were doubtless procured from England, and China or Ware of quality of the broken Specimen was made, but to what extent I cannot say: However the news was soon conveyed to England that the manufacture had commenced, when speedily arrived cargoes of the English or Dutch Ware sufficient to supply the demand of the Colony or Colonies. Unable to withstand the competition with the manufacturers in Europe, Mr. Bonnin ceased his labors. The dinner set of his China was all that my father ever got for his £500. The quality of it was about equal to the Delft ware of Holland of which much of the American table sets was composed and which was first imported into England previously to being sent to this Country, the direct trade being prohibited.

This letter was written seventy years after the factory closed. Read critically, it is far from reassuring. Dr. Mease was not exactly sure of the precise area of Philadelphia in which the factory was situated, despite a proclaimed connection between his father and Bonnin. He was not exactly sure, either, of the origin of the workmen for the factory and the extent of production. His qualitative comparison of the fruit basket with delft was unfortunate, and casts the strongest doubts on his ability to distinguish between various kinds of ceramics. The most striking discord, however, appeared in connection with the mark on the object; this is an underglaze blue "P", whereas Bonnin and Morris, in announcing their first production of porcelain in January 1771, included in the advertisement the following statement: "To prevent retail purchasers being imposed upon, they are desired to take notice, all future emissions from this factory will be marked S." Scholars have hitherto explained away this anomaly by conjecturing that the "S" in the newspaper advertisement might be a printer's error. Such an explanation is simplistic, for the advertisement appeared in three different Pennsylvania newspapers in the same month and ran in each one for two or three issues. The partners could not have failed to correct any misinformation about the marking of the wares at this critical early period.

Despite these strictures, however, Dr. Mease's letter does contain some correct information. He was obviously familiar with Bonnin's antecedents and accurately described the main building of the factory. His assumption that the workmen came from England proves correct, and the reasons he gave for the failure of the factory are acceptable. Furthermore, his notation of the source of the clay is confirmed in one other, apparently independent, statement.

What transpired, therefore, was that the documentary evidence was as ambiguous as the technical—and, in fact, as the stylistic. The piece in question is a shallow bowl with straight sides consisting of openwork interlaced circles joined by horizontal struts and with small molded flowers applied on the outside at each juncture. It is closely related to English baskets, particularly Lowestoft, which were modeled after Worcester prototypes. The paste has a distinctive porridge-like texture and has turned yellowish brown where not glazed. Many impurities are in the glaze, which was obviously intractable enough to form numerous, thick, greenish blue pools all over the piece, with a wavy crackelure. The glaze also blurs and obscures the painted flowers and leaves design. On this basket is painted a typical Lowestoft motif of a scrolled band on the inside of the lip (fig. 22).[41] In addition, the molded flowers on the outside resemble those on the base of an unpainted Lowestoft figure (Watney Collection). Two octagonal saucers with unmarked tea bowls (Watney Collection), marked with a similar "P", were made at Longton Hall.[42]

Another fruit basket attributed to Bonnin and Morris is also marked with a "P" (figs. 5–7). Somewhat larger and more assured in technique, it is even more thickly potted than the Philadelphia fruit basket and, like it, is not at all translucent. The glaze is slightly more refined, although it has still flowed unevenly and is still bubbly with pitting. The painted decoration on the flowers and on the rim is more assured. It is transfer-printed inside—a mode of decoration popular in England from the 1760s, although it certainly could have been done at the Bonnin and Morris factory; among the sale effects of the factory was listed "a rolling press for copper-plate printing." This print closely resembles the print on a cup formerly thought to be Lowestoft (fig. 23) and now reattributed to Bow. This print also appeared on Lowestoft from about 1770 onward, but was not, apparently, used on baskets such as this; the print was also used at Worcester. The basket, now in the Winterthur Museum, was acquired from a direct descendant of Morris's uncle, John Morris (1709–1782).

Despite the similarities to Lowestoft, the straight sides of the fruit baskets and the precise type of applied molded flower are not common in Lowestoft porcelain.[43] The English equivalent of the print used on the Winterthur piece generally contains an idiosyncratic cross in the center of each flower, which does not occur on the fruit basket. Finally, the major collection of Lowestoft porcelain in England (Castle Museum, Norwich) contains not a single piece marked with "P".

The large sauceboat and the sweetmeats dish in the Brooklyn Museum (figs. 8–9, 11–13) are marked "P" and, on this basis, have been attributed to Bonnin and Morris. The sweetmeats dish is perhaps the most ornate form among the group and could be the "pickle-stand" referred to in the Wharton and Cadwalader bills as the most expensive item there. Here the paste retains its porridge-like texture, although both objects are more thinly potted than the fruit baskets. Molded ornament is used extensively, as a raised pattern on the body and foot of the sauceboat and on the various shells of the sweetmeats dish. This glaze is slightly grayish blue and does not collect so heavily in thick pools, but it still contains many impurities. There are also small areas the glaze has not covered or where a large bubble in the glaze burst in the firing; here the body has turned yellowish brown. Under strong light both objects show a slight, underfired, brownish yellow translucency with a few small moons. Both objects contain more than 10 percent phosphate.

The sauceboat is painted with pseudo-Chinese scenes and bears a general resemblance to the products of Chaffers's Liverpool factory (1754–1765). Such details as the sprigs of leaves, the trees, the rocks, and the inside border all occur on

Chaffers's wares.[44] The painted scene on the side is very similar to that on a salt, dated 1767, made in the same factory after Chaffers's death by Philip Christian (fig. 24). The handle resembles a Liverpool handle of about 1756–1760.[45] Yet most Chaffers's Liverpool wares are steatitic rather than phosphatic, and sauceboats from that factory are generally much better molded. Illustrative of the danger of overemphatic conclusions in this area is the resemblance of motifs on this same sauceboat—the shape of the rim, the flower below the handle inside, and the molded and painted shell on the inside and outside of the rim—to Bow (fig. 25). At first sight the sweetmeats dish evokes comparison with Bow (fig. 26). However, the molding of the shells and the form of the twig ends strongly resembles Derby blue and white.[46] It is painted inside each of its shells with a scene similar to the print on the Philadelphia fruit basket (figs. 3, 12).

Completing this small group are a small, shell-shaped tray in the Philadelphia Museum of Art (fig. 10), an openwork dish in the Yale University Art Gallery (figs. 20–21), and two small fluted sauceboats of identical size, the more complete one of which only recently appeared (figs. 14–15, 27–29). These are notable for the thinner, molded bodies and the grayish blue, slightly bubbly glaze with many impurities. Here, too, the glaze either "dragged" or pitted deeply in the firing. All are translucent under strong light, the openwork dish and the sauceboats noticeably so. They are less phosphatic than the other examples, although the spot tests gave positive indications of rather more than 2 percent phosphatic content. The recently discovered sauceboat (figs. 27–29) is decorated with an identical scene to that on the Brooklyn sauceboat, with the same dotted, diamond-border motif inside the rim, and identical sprigs of leaves over the surface. On the inside rim under the handle and under the spout are almost identical painted floral pendants. As we have seen, this motif was used at Liverpool and at Bow, while the sprigs of leaves can be seen on a small fluted Lowestoft sauceboat.[47] The other small sauceboat (figs. 14–15) appears to be close to later Bow, although the paste has none of the characteristic Bow tears. Nor is it so fine as late Bow, which is not notable for its high quality. It also utilizes the dotted, diamond-border motif inside the spout, but it has a different pendant border design inside the flutes and floral sprays rather than sprigs of leaves over the body. The painted scene, less assured and interesting than the other sauceboat, is identical to that on the small, shell-shaped pickle tray. Such trays with conical feet— the same kind of feet as those on the picklestand—are unusual in English blue and white, although they do occur on Bow and occasionally on Pennington's Liverpool wares. Furthermore, most English shells have the painted scene facing the squared rather than the rounded end. The Yale openwork dish is a hitherto unknown form in English blue and white. In general character it appears to be close to Derby, yet base decoration of this type was common at Bow earlier.[48] The main band of painted cell work was used by various English factories after 1760.

After the conclusion of the archaeological project more pieces closely related to this group came to light, and are most conveniently discussed here. Three of them had descended in Philadelphia families. Two fruit baskets (figs. 30–34) came from the Whitehead family and are presumably a pair, although the scenes inside vary in slight details. Not only are the baskets identical to the Philadelphia Museum example in form, but the underglaze blue decoration is also very similar. The two baskets are slightly larger than the single one, being more akin in this respect, as in their fairly high degree of quality, to the Winterthur example, which is, of course, transfer-printed. Apart from the self-evident family likeness between all these fruit baskets—the kind of paste and glaze, the character of the flowers, the footring—there is one slight difference; the pair of fruit baskets is marked with an underglaze blue "S" backwards, or "Z". This was the first intimation among the known surviving wares that Bonnin and Morris might have marked some of their products with the mark "S", as they announced in their advertisement of January 1771 that they intended to do. Presumably the letter "S" was for Southwark, where the factory was located; it was, therefore, only a slight change to "P", presumably for Philadelphia or Pennsylvania, and since the wares were still very similar the partners may have decided not to announce such a change. In any event, these marks may have been used interchangeably throughout the period of production.

Another openwork dish (potpourri dish?), perhaps the most elaborate form yet known, recently appeared (figs. 35–36). Its body is identical in form to the Yale dish, even to the three molded rings below the openwork. This example, however, has an elaborate cover with a knop in the form of a flower. It is not so precisely decorated as the Yale piece. An underglaze "P" appears under both dish and cover. The dish was acquired by Catherine Deshler of Philadelphia at about the time of her marriage in 1775 to Robert Roberts, and descended directly in the Roberts and Canby families.

Shortly before this book went to press yet another piece of porcelain and some interesting shards appeared (fig. 37). The piece is identical to the Brooklyn Museum sweetmeats dish in form (figs. 11–13), although it is finer in execution. The painted designs inside the shells differ slightly, being very close to the fine fruit baskets (figs. 30–34). It is unmarked. The shards (fig. 38) came from the excavations at Hanna's Town in Westmoreland County, Pennsylvania, a settlement founded about 1769–1773 on the main route between Philadelphia and Fort Pitt (Pittsburgh). The settlement was one day's ride east of Fort Pitt and reached a fair size before it was

burned by the Indians and British in 1782. A close relationship between the design on the shards (which are from a flat
inside surface such as the bottom of a fruit basket) and
that on the Winterthur basket (fig. 5) is obvious. Furthermore, the shards were analyzed by x-ray diffraction and
proved to be identical in composition to those already tested.
One of the shards is actually marked with an "S"—the only
announced factory mark but, in fact, the third one to appear
up to the present time.

Intensive examination of all the available evidence thus
produced no decisive answer to the main questions. In composition the wares were not distinct from certain English
wares. Stylistically, there were some internal correspondences
but also a great many similarities to the wares of several English factories. And the documentary evidence was not clear
enough to confirm or deny that the one important object was
of Philadelphia manufacture, as purported. The field of English blue and white porcelain is so large and intricate and so
much new material is continually coming to light that, from
a diligent and critical point of view, further concrete evidence
was necessary before it could be said that this small group
was of separate and distinct origin. Obviously, this evidence
could only be obtained from the factory site.

Sanguinity, perseverance, and fortune went hand in hand.
In the summer of 1967, tests were performed on the site of
the factory. Of a dozen test trenches sunk, eleven proved
totally negative; below a shallow layer of fairly recent detritus
appeared, in each case, undisturbed yellow clay. The evidence
of these trenches seemed to indicate that the ground was hilly
in the late eighteenth century and had been leveled at some
time since the demise of the factory. Although these trenches
were disappointingly empty, the final test was very positive.
Immediately beneath the surface detritus a profuse layer of
sagger fragments was uncovered (figs. 39–40). With these

saggers were mingled some unglazed fragments of a ceramic body. Such was the quality of form and content of these latter that it was difficult to believe they were anything other than a soft-paste porcelain. Samples sent to the British Museum proved this contention; not only were these unglazed fragments composed of elements similar to those wares already tested (figs. 1, 20), but it was also found that they contained relatively coarse particles of alpha-quartz, in common with the Yale openwork dish. This is a factor not commonly encountered in English soft-paste, bone-ash porcelain; it should be noted that pieces of quartz were later dug from the site and quartz particles were also found sprinkled on the inside bottom of some saggers.

Fortuitously, this test trench was situated in the backyard of a demolished house. With the kind owner's permission to proceed with the excavation, and armed with the samples of evidence from the site, it was possible to approach members of the Morris family and a philanthropic organization in Philadelphia for support for an excavation, on the supposition that there must be more evidence readily accessible. Both responded with great generosity, and work began on this small but choice (and available) site in the fall of 1967. With appropriate interruption during the winter, the work continued until the early summer of 1968.

Hedged in by city streets, private dwellings, businesses, and a multitude of sundry impedimenta (figs. 41–42), the area available for excavation was restricted—approximately two hundred square feet. Bounded on the south and east sides by private properties, on the west side by an old coal yard, and on the north by the foundations of a brick house (replete with cellar) that had been recently demolished, this lot was so small as to prohibit anything more than three six-foot squares to be sunk. The area was slightly to the north, and at the west end, of where the main building of the factory had been (figs. 16 and 19) and was, therefore, between the main building and the "kilns, furnaces, cisterns, engines," and other structures mentioned in the sales notices.

Excavation disclosed the fact that the mid-eighteenth-century topsoil level was buried by kiln waste (mainly saggers and unglazed fragments) and various other disposables (decorated and glazed shards and low-fired clay fragments) from the Bonnin and Morris factory (fig. 43). Domestic refuse of a normal type was later deposited on, and worked into, this stratum for several decades after the factory closed and the property divided. To this was added approximately six inches of topsoil fill, containing waste similar to that dating from the period of the factory's activity; the most likely source for this layer was the excavation for the cellar of the house, built about 1825. Later additions to the house covered part of the area excavated. In the late nineteenth century the entire backyard, now containing many creamware, ironstone, stoneware, and earthenware fragments, was paved with brick. A few years ago this layer was covered with concrete.

Within a few years of the factory's closing, a pit for a privy was dug through the layer of factory waste in the northeast corner of the area. This was filled ca. 1780 and supplemented a little later when the contents settled. Included in this original fill were parts of wine bottles and part of a square case bottle, a complete Staffordshire, salt-glazed stoneware saucer with scratch decoration in blue (fig. 44), a fine creamware cup, two earthenware bowls with white slip decoration inside, a small earthenware cup or porringer with a black glaze (fig. 45), and a fragment of a large, dark, salt-glazed stoneware jar bearing the incised mark of "CARR & ROBERTS," potters who worked in or near the factory buildings between 1774 and 1784 (see note 34). In the later fill of the privy appeared painted pearlware, which was not present in the earlier fill. The area was later disturbed by a large brick cesspit and two privies, with brickbat paving in front, at the southeast corner of the lot. In recent years postholes and a trench for a soil pipe were further cut into the area.

Because there was only one object in the small group of wares attributed to Bonnin and Morris—the Philadelphia Museum fruit basket—whose documentary connection with the factory was anything other than tangential, we were especially concerned to find some archaeological reference to it. Evidence was not long in forthcoming. Some unglazed and some low-fired fragments of the type of molded flower applied to the pierced sides of the fruit basket were found (fig. 46). These fragments were identical in character to those on the finished piece (fig. 47). The previous scale of evidence was thus heavily tipped in favor of the old attribution of this piece to Bonnin and Morris. Among the first shards appeared transfer-printed fragments bearing a design identical to that on the Winterthur fruit basket, which, of course, is so similar to the Philadelphia piece (figs. 48–49). One of these fragments bore the print on a convex surface, probably the side of a sugar bowl, in contrast to the flat surface of the other shards and of the fruit basket itself.

Shards also came to light that were identical to parts of the scene painted on the Philadelphia pickle tray and the small broken sauceboat: the tall reeds at the left of the scene, and the trunk and coarsely painted foliage at upper center (fig. 50). Among the unglazed shards were many molded pieces, some of which obviously came from the same mold as the Brooklyn sauceboat (fig. 51, nos. 1, 4). The most attractive shard found was part of a quilted cup with a painted cell design at the lip (fig. 52, no. 3), so similar to a Bow example of the 1760s.[49] We know that the factory made quilted cups, for they are listed in the Wharton bill, and many fragments of this type turned up (fig. 52). The painted cell work of this shard is exactly identical in character to that on the

Yale openwork dish (figs. 20–21). Even at this stage, there-fore, it was quite apparent that, together with the internal cor-respondences previously noted with the group of wares, the evidence of the shards resoundingly endorsed the traditional attribution of this whole group of objects to the Bonnin and Morris factory.

A particularly significant shard appeared in the form of a tiny fragment of the footring of a saucer, decorated inside with an underglaze iron red scene of houses and trees (fig. 53, left). Such is the occidental character of this fragment of a scene that one is tempted to believe it may have formed part of a local view. The partners had advertised complete sets of dressing boxes with enameled decoration in January 1772, and it may well be that underglaze red (highly unusual in technique) was their version of "enamelled wares." It is also possible that in the remaining months they used this mode of decoration on useful wares too. Another fragment from a saucer footring with underglaze red decoration appeared (fig. 53, right), as well as a part of a punch bowl footring that bore faint traces of red inside.[50]

Almost all of the shards are so small that it is difficult to deduce anything further from them, particularly in reference to other scenes and types of decoration that the factory used but that have not survived. Various kinds and sizes of border designs appeared. Fragments of scenes are almost all of rocks, trees, and similar details, in the pseudo-Chinese manner.

Shards of molded wares, virtually all unglazed and some low-fired, prove that the quality of this type of object was surprisingly high; a sample is shown in fig. 51. The orna-mentation of a small group shown here (fig. 51, no. 4), remarkably precise and attractively designed, surely reverses the previous contention that the Bonnin and Morris wares

were merely of a second-rate, provincial order. Fragments
nos. 2 and 3 in this small group seem to be from a mold for a
small sauceboat with scrolled decoration on its sides and a
scalloped rim. Several sizes and thicknesses of the quilted
pattern were found, including saucer footrings quilted inside; the number of these shards may point to the popularity
of this pattern in Philadelphia at the time. Other molded
fragments included pieces of handles similar to those on the
sauceboats; a finial of a sugar bowl or teapot; scalloped rims;
part of a shell similar to those on the Brooklyn centerpiece
or the Philadelphia pickle tray; parts of crucibles; and what
may be the spout juncture of a teapot.

Fragments of footrings and rims abound in the evidence
from the site; all of these are finely, and some beautifully,
made. Two varieties of cup footrings appeared (fig. 54, nos.
1–2), the first of which has traces of the quilted pattern above.
They measure $1^{11}\!/_{32}''$ and $1\frac{1}{2}''$ in diameter. These cup fragments were found mainly in the dark brown, sandy loam
layer (later deposited on the sagger—or refuse discarded by
the factory—layer about 1825, when the house was built and
a hole dug for its cellar). Cup rims form an arc within a
compass-drawn circle $3\frac{1}{2}''$ in diameter; this gives us, of
course, the original size of the object. The quilted cup rim is
$3\frac{3}{16}''$ in diameter.

Saucer fragments (fig. 56), again very precisely made, also
appeared predominantly in the dark brown, sandy loam layer,
although more rims were found in the sagger layer. Foot-
rings measure $3''$ and $3\frac{1}{4}''$ in diameter and rims $5\frac{1}{4}''$. As with
the cups, approximately twice as many unglazed or unfired
fragments of saucers were found as the glazed and/or decorated pieces.

Plate footrings (fig. 56) measuring $4^{13}\!/_{32}''$ in diameter, none
of which are glazed, came from the dark brown, sandy loam

layer. From these footrings and a part of a rim it is possible to estimate a diameter of 8½″ for the plate. No evidence of different-sized plates appeared.

Small bowl rims, and what is probably the footring for such a vessel, turned up in both layers in approximately equal quantities. Only one fragment is glazed. The rim is 4½″ in diameter and the footring 2²³⁄₃₂″. This type of bowl may have been a sugar or slop bowl. Some of the large bowl footrings, almost 4″ in diameter, were presumably part of the punch bowls of four- and six-quart capacity advertised shortly after the first production of porcelain occurred.

It is interesting to note that a higher proportion of recognizable cup and saucer fragments came from the sagger layer than from the dark brown sandy loam, and a higher proportion of these are glazed and sometimes decorated. This may mean that this type of object, presumably the most commonly made, was the last type of ware to be made at the factory, or that the various kilns of the factory were designed for different types of wares and the excavation site was near the kiln in which the smaller wares were fired.

The unglazed shards are of a surprisingly high degree of quality. Apart from the mention already made of molded pieces and footrings, an outstanding feature of many of the fragments of smaller objects is their actual thinness. Such rims and edges, frequently painted with border designs, are often only ⅓₂″ thick and could not conceivably have withstood extended usage. Much of the porcelain, indeed, is quixotically thin and surely accounts for some of the contemporary criticism of the quality of the wares.

Great quantities of saggers were dug from the site. They constitute two groups, one made with a pink fire-clay, which is by far the most numerous, the other of a somewhat finer yellow clay. Both types were tempered with quartz and mica granules, which may well have been spread on the inside bottom of the sagger to provide a rough surface, into which excess glaze could drip without flooding the bottom of the sagger and on top of which the trivets or stilts could stand. A fragment of a pink sagger (illustrated in the center of fig. 55) was found with such a granular layer below a green glaze; a T-shaped prop and a fragment of porcelain can be seen fused to the bottom of the sagger by the glaze.

Saggers of pink clay were formed by the wheel-turned sides being pressed on to a flat, round bottom; the clay was obviously wet when sides and bottom were joined since impressions of the workmen's fingers are frequently visible. Before the sagger was fired it was turned again, the sides being smoothed off and made thinner and the top edge cut level. These saggers measure 8½″ to 14½″ in diameter and are from 2¾″ to over 8″ in height; the sides vary from ⅝″ to ¾″ in thickness (Appendix 15). Most of the saggers are 13″ in diameter; they were presumably stacked on top of each other in the kiln since nothing that could be called a lid for this size was found. The glaze that gathered on the inside of many of the pink clay saggers in the firing has a distinctive green color.

Several examples of open-ended cylinders of this same clay, 13″ in diameter, also turned up; they range from 2″ to 2¾″ in height and were presumably used as extension tubes on top of the regular saggers. Many fragments of smaller, flat, round disks of pink clay were found, about ¾″ thick and between 4″ and 5″ in diameter. They seem to have been cut by a compass, as there is often a tiny hole in the center. Although they are all highly fired, none of the disks bears any traces of glaze, and it is possible that they were used in the first firing only.

In general, the yellow clay saggers present a smoother and neater appearance than the pink. Although a few are similar in design and size to the pink, most were thrown and turned in a single operation, with sides and bottoms of uneven thickness and shape; the sides of these saggers varied from ⅜″ to 1″ in a single object, while the bottom was sometimes as thin as ¼″. Occasionally the upper rim of this type is thickened or flared. These saggers range from 8½″ to 14½″ in diameter and from 3½″ to 4¼″ in height. Several of these yellow sagger walls had triangular holes cut in them, from 1½″ to 4″ below the rim, presumably to allow the insertion of pins to support plates. Large flat disks of the same clay seem to have been used to cover the saggers, since they are of a similar diameter and are coated with the brownish glaze that characterizes this group (only four pieces of these covers were found, however). They are irregular in outline, so that when placed on top of a sagger they would touch the rim at only three or four places.

Among the other kiln furniture found were three varieties of kiln props, trivets, or stilts; one is T-shaped, another circular, and a third rod-shaped (fig. 55). In contrast to the precision of the circular props, the former kinds were quite roughly made. The T-shaped props were formed by hand of white-burning clay, being triangular in cross section and not more than three inches in length. The rod-shaped props are of pink or yellow clay and are the same length; they have been somewhat flattened on two sides, and one end is rounded while the other end is broken. These were probably used to support objects such as bowls or plates in the first firing. Ring props came in many sizes. Carefully turned, these props invariably have a thin edge with a recess facing outside, perhaps to support another ring. Fig. 55 also shows a reconstructed part of a sagger with indentations for the ring props and part of a fused T-shaped prop above. At the bottom of this illustration can be seen a fragment of pugging clay used to seal the tops of stacked saggers. A layer of quartz granules, mentioned above, was frequently, but not invariably, scattered in the bottom of the sagger.

From such a limited site it is obviously difficult to draw major archaeological conclusions; indeed, this particular project was undertaken in the hope of proving only one thing, which it certainly did. Urban archaeology has ever had to contend with problems of encroachment, in the form of private enterprise building houses with cellars, digging huge holes in the ground in modern times to store fuel to heat those houses, and constructing various devices to carry sewage away from houses. Public enterprise has followed hard upon —railroads, tramways, city streets, and, most recently and devastatingly, and holier than mere history, expressways. It is miraculous that, between each and every vagary mentioned above, a small remnant of the eighteenth-century porcelain factory survived underground in this one available area.

Because of the disturbances most of the sagger fragments and shards were small in size, and few of the pieces could be matched together. It would seem that most of the material found here was spillover from the site of an original waste pit or was moved here shortly after the factory closed. It is possible that the site was near the first-firing kiln, which might account for the high proportion of unglazed to glazed pieces. It is also possible that the original waste pits survive, either to the east on private property or to the north under Washington Avenue. Tests made in the coal yard to the west proved totally negative. It is worth recording that, according to a local account, excavations for fuel tanks within recent years disclosed a great number of bones and, in a slightly different location, a large pit of fine clay, probably the factory's puddling pit.

Devoted as they were in their attentions to the Bonnin and Morris factory, the various historians of American ceramics cited at the beginning of this book can hardly be said to have presented a clear or convincing account of the factory's activities. Considerably more succinct, but perhaps less charitable, the author of the brilliant and definitive history of English blue and white porcelain of the eighteenth century dismissed the factory in a couple of lines. Confusion or neglect need not continue. Scientific tests performed on shards found on the site of the factory prove that Bonnin and Morris made soft-paste porcelain. Most of this seems to have been painted or transfer-printed in underglaze blue; the partners' ambitions went beyond this, however, in attempting the manufacture of enameled wares too. With admittedly small initial capacities, the partners appear to have made a creditable attempt to launch a significant enterprise. That their endeavor was not negligible may be seen in the interest and patronage of wealthy Philadelphians of the time; the author of the previously quoted "Memoir of Thomas Gilpin" concluded his description of the factory thus: "A number of beautiful articles particularly of tea ware well shaped and painted were in use among the best families in America." It need not surprise anyone conversant with the history of European ceramics in this period that the factory failed. In any event, it would hardly have survived the vicissitudes of the impending Revolutionary War.

The small group of useful, soft-paste porcelain wares that survives today can now be proved, rather than wishfully believed, to have been made by Bonnin and Morris. In this case the traditional attribution proved to be correct, but the initial doubts led to the eventual discovery of much more extensive and exciting evidence of the factory's activities than a mere acceptance of an old attribution would have done. More of the finished wares undoubtedly remain in or near Philadelphia and will presumably appear in the future. It may well be that the evidence from the site of the factory, now given in toto to the Philadelphia Museum of Art, will help to verify some of these pieces. In quality the known pieces range from the commendable to the mediocre. Presumably, in such a short time and with limited means, it was impossible for the partners to think in other than predominantly commercial terms. Yet it should be acknowledged that the wares were fashionably up to date, for styles appeared here within a decade of their introduction in England—exactly the same kind of interval that marks the transmission of particular style innovations in silver from England to the colonies. The floral and foliate motifs, especially those in relief, the scrolled molded decoration, the pierced work, and the shells employed in this porcelain are precisely the motifs that characterize the contemporary work of three of the finest silversmiths active in America at this time, Richardson, Myers, and Revere. The amalgam of decorative motifs found in the known wares is no different from contemporary English porcelain factories; these were culled from the various factories that the workmen had, according to the character of their profession, drifted into and out of. Nevertheless, these few pieces do form a distinct group within the various British eighteenth-century blue and white porcelains, and the factory is important as the unique American porcelain factory of the colonial period of which significant evidence survives.

1. Fruit basket. Bonnin and Morris, 1771–1772. Soft-paste porcelain, painted in underglaze blue. H. 2"; D. 6".

Philadelphia Museum of Art, Philadelphia, Pa.

2. Side view of fig. 1.

3. Inside view of fig. 1.

4. "P" mark on fig. 1.

5. Fruit basket. Bonnin and Morris, 1771–1772. Soft-paste porcelain, painted and transfer-printed in underglaze blue. H. 2⅝"; D. 8⅛".

Henry Francis du Pont Winterthur Museum, Wilmington, Del.

6. Side view of fig. 5.

7. "P" mark on fig. 5.

8. Sauceboat. Bonnin and Morris, 1771–1772. Soft-paste porcelain, painted in underglaze blue. H. 4"; L. 7⅜"; W. 3½".

Brooklyn Museum, Brooklyn, N.Y.

9. "P" mark on fig. 8.

10. Shell-shaped pickle tray. Bonnin and Morris, 1771–1772. Soft-paste porcelain, painted in underglaze blue. H. 1¼"; D. 4½".

Philadelphia Museum of Art, Philadelphia, Pa.

11. Sweetmeats dish. Bonnin and Morris, 1771–1772. Soft-paste porcelain, painted in underglaze blue. H. 5¼″; D. 7¼″.

Brooklyn Museum, Brooklyn, N.Y.

12. Inside view of fig. 11.

13. "P" mark on fig. 11.

*14. Sauceboat. Bonnin and Morris, 1771–1772. Soft-paste porcelain,
painted in underglaze blue. H. 2¼"; L. 3⅞".*

Mrs. George K. Stout, on loan to the Metropolitan Museum of Art,
New York, N.Y.

15. "P" mark on fig. 14.

16. View of Southwark, from the John Hills map of Philadelphia, 1796.

Newcastle Lottery,

Instituted by the Friends of the

American China Manufactory,

For the Purpose of raising the clear Sum of.... £4500
3393.15
£1106.5:—

One Thousand Pounds,

Towards the Encouragement of the said Manufactory. —

Scheme of the Lottery.

One Prize of *Two Thousand* Dollars.	2000
One Prize of One Thousand Ditto.	1000
One Prize of Four Hundred Ditto.	400
Two Prizes of One Hundred Ditto.	200
Three Prizes of Fifty Ditto.	150
Five Prizes of Twenty Ditto.	100
One Thousand and Twenty Prizes of Five Ditto.	5100
One Ticket, first drawn, will be Forty Ditto.	40
One Ticket, last drawn, will be Sixty Ditto.	60

9050 = £3393.15.

1035 Prizes.
1965 Blanks.
———
3000 Tickets. a 30/ — £4500

For the Encouragement of Adventurers, it may be observed, that there are not Two Blanks to a Prize.

Immediately on publishing a List of fortunate Numbers the Prizes shall be paid,

Free from any Deduction.

As a great Number of Tickets are already engaged by the Friends of this Manufactory, and the Managers have the greatest Certainty that they shall be enabled punctually to draw, on the *Tenth* Day of *August* next, at *Christiana Bridge:* They request such Persons, as incline to become Adventurers in this Lottery, will be speedy in making Application.

Orders for Tickets, sent to the *China Manufactory,* or left at the *Barr* of the *London Coffee-House* in *Philadelphia,* will immediately be forwarded.

Tickets, at *Thirty Shillings* each, are sold by *TOBIAS RUDULPH,* Esq; and Mr. *SAMUEL PATTERSON,* Managers; who are upon Oath for the faithful Discharge of the Trust reposed in them.

17. Announcement of lottery in aid of the Bonnin and Morris factory, 1771.

Library Company of Philadelphia, Philadelphia, Pa.

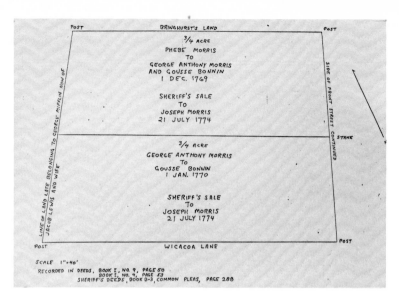

18. Details of property ownership for the Bonnin and Morris factory site.

Drawn by Paul R. Huey.

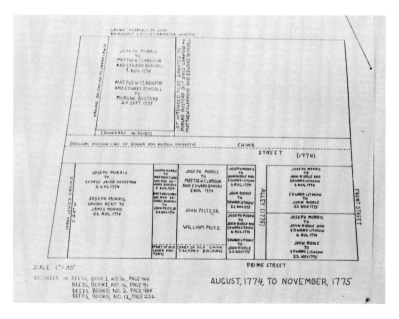

19. Details of property ownership for the Bonnin and Morris factory site after the closing of the factory.

Drawn by Paul R. Huey.

20. *Openwork dish. Bonnin and Morris, 1771–1772. Soft-paste porcelain,
painted in underglaze blue. H. 2½"; D. 3¹¹⁄₁₆".*

Yale University Art Gallery, New Haven, Conn.

21. *"P" mark on fig. 20.*

22. Tureen and saucer. Lowestoft, ca. 1760–1765. Soft-paste porcelain, painted in underglaze blue. H. (tureen) 4"; L. (saucer) 7".

Victoria and Albert Museum, London.

23. Cup and jug. Bow, ca. 1765–1770. Soft-paste porcelain, transfer-printed in underglaze blue. H. (cup) 2⅜".

Watney Collection, London.

24. Inkwell. Philip Christian's Liverpool factory, dated 1767. Soft-paste porcelain, painted in underglaze blue. H. 2¼"; D. 2¾".

Victoria and Albert Museum, London.

25. Sauceboat. Bow, ca. 1765. Soft-paste porcelain, painted in underglaze blue. H. 3¾"; L. 7⅞".

Victoria and Albert Museum, London.

26. Sweetmeats dish. Bow, ca. 1765. Soft-paste porcelain, painted in under-glaze blue. H. 5"; D. 6¾".

Victoria and Albert Museum, London.

27. *Sauceboat. Bonnin and Morris, 1771–1772. Soft-paste porcelain, painted in underglaze blue. H. 2¼"; L. 4⅝".*

Private collection, Philadelphia, Pa.

28. Front view of fig. 27.

29. "P" mark on fig. 27.

30. Fruit basket. Bonnin and Morris, 1771–1772. Soft-paste porcelain, painted in underglaze blue. D. 6⅞".

Dr. Horace G. Richards and Miss Marie Richards, Philadelphia, Pa.

31. "Z" mark on fig. 30.

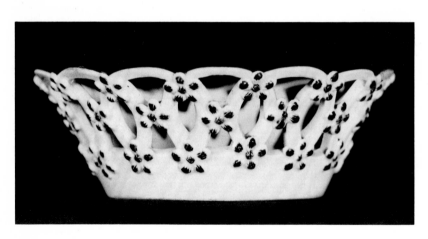

32. Side view of fig. 30.

33. Fruit basket. Bonnin and Morris, 1771–1772. Soft-paste porcelain, painted in underglaze blue. D. 6⅞".

Gibbs-Williams Fund, Detroit Institute of Arts, Detroit, Mich.

34. "Z" mark on fig. 33.

35. Covered openwork dish. Bonnin and Morris, 1771–1772. Soft-paste porcelain, painted in underglaze blue. H. 3¾"; D. 4⅛".

The Colonial Williamsburg Foundation, Williamsburg, Va.

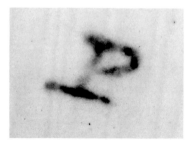

36. "P" mark on body of fig. 35.

37. Inside view of sweetmeats dish. Bonnin and Morris, 1771–1772. Soft-paste porcelain, painted in underglaze blue. H. 5½".

Gift of the Barra Foundation; Smithsonian Institution, Washington, D.C.

38. Shards from the old Hanna's Town site, Westmoreland County, Pennsylvania.

Westmoreland County Historical Society, and Carnegie Museum, Pittsburgh, Pa.

39. Sagger finds in the test trench.

40. Wasters exposed in the test trench.

41. View of the site of the excavation, October 1967, taken from the north.

42. View of the excavation in progress, October 1967, facing slightly southeast.

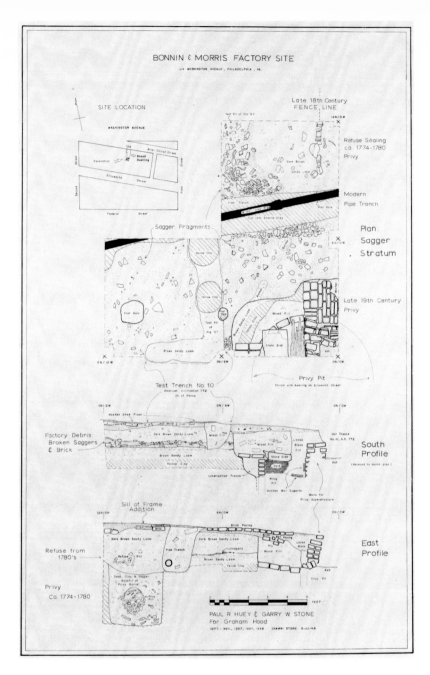

43. Details of the outline and profiles of the excavation.
Drawn by Garry Wheeler Stone.

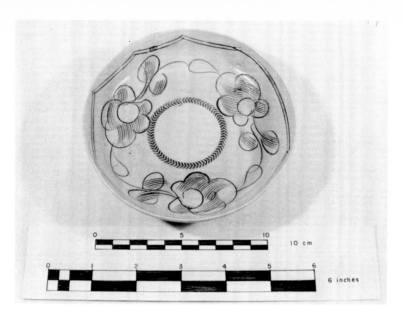

44. Saucer. Staffordshire, ca. 1780. Salt-glazed stoneware, scratch-decorated in blue. Taken from the site of the excavation.

Philadelphia Museum of Art, Philadelphia, Pa.

45. Cup or porringer. Earthenware, late eighteenth century. Taken from the site of the excavation.

Philadelphia Museum of Art, Philadelphia, Pa.

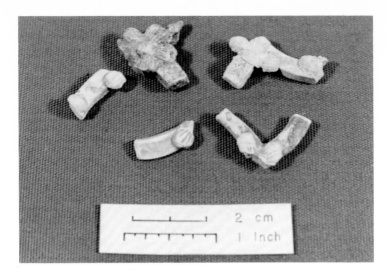

46. Unglazed and unfired shards. Bonnin and Morris, 1771–1772. Soft-paste porcelain.

Philadelphia Museum of Art, Philadelphia, Pa.

47. Relationship of the shards in fig. 46 to the fruit basket in figs. 1–4.

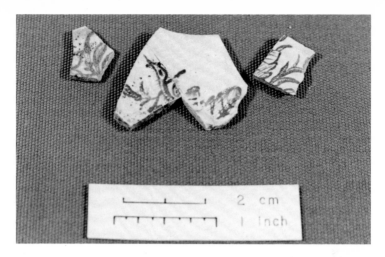

48. Transfer-printed shards. Bonnin and Morris, 1771–1772. Soft-paste porcelain.

Philadelphia Museum of Art, Philadelphia, Pa.

49. Relationship of the shards in fig. 48 to the fruit basket in figs. 5–7.

50. Relationship of the shards to the pickle tray in fig. 10.

51. Unglazed molded shards. Bonnin and Morris, 1771–1772. Soft-paste porcelain.

Philadelphia Museum of Art, Philadelphia, Pa.

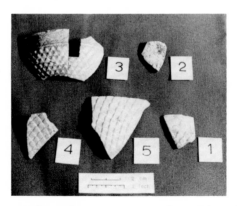

52. Fragments of the quilted pattern. Bonnin and Morris, 1771–1772. Soft-paste porcelain.

Philadelphia Museum of Art, Philadelphia, Pa.

53. Fragments with underglaze red decoration. Bonnin and Morris, 1771–1772. Soft-paste porcelain.

Philadelphia Museum of Art, Philadelphia, Pa.

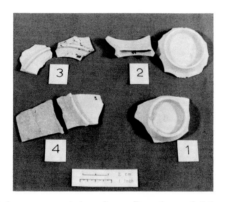

54. Unglazed fragments of footrings. Bonnin and Morris, 1771–1772. Soft-paste porcelain.

Philadelphia Museum of Art, Philadelphia, Pa.

55. Fragments of kiln furniture. Bonnin and Morris factory site.

Philadelphia Museum of Art, Philadelphia, Pa.

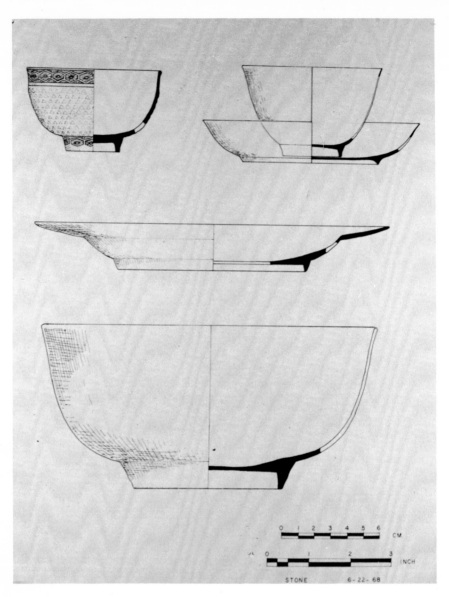

56. Cross sections of wares. Bonnin and Morris, 1771–1772. Dark areas show relevant shards found.

Drawn by Garry Wheeler Stone.

Appendixes

———◆•◆———

APPENDIX 1

                                        Antigua September 21st 1770

To Sir Charles Palmer

Dear Sir

    Your favor of 28th May I received two Nights ago and Note the Contents full well Wish with all my Heart Could Gratefie your desire when you Know my reason beleive you will not Blame me; first then I settled on Gousse two Tennements renting for £366 per Annum, upon which he settled his Wife's Jointer Adequate to Her Fortune. but Neither takes place till After yours and my Death, but to theirs and my Misfortune are boath Consumed by Fire, this Misfortune reduces my income of £366 two Other Tennements renting at the Same £366 Consumed at the Same time, Which I intended for my Daughter; who has three Children may have many More God Only Knows, Lays in Rubish; Secondly Gousse On his Arrival at Philadelphia Borrowed £600, in his absence to England Mrs. Bonnin borrowed £100 more, for this £700 I am paying Interest at Philadelphia; When in England He took up £280 Sterl. immediately, after his return Drew Bills upon Messrs. Oliver for £200 which they very Kindly paid: and since for £520. 12. 2 am not yett Certain of more than £250 paid; but hope my Letter of Advice to pay them will Arrive in time to prevent A protest. all which I am under Obligation to pay with Interest to Support his Credit in his New Scheme, al this he has done without previous advice to me, and was a thousand to one had not

                                [47]

bin his Ruin, and Mine to. and am still fearfull may be the Case
as I have not heard from him since the 8th of July, all was well then
in his famly. I have Made Some repairs for my owne Occupation
at the place Called Duers, and am Building A large store where
we Called White Hall when finished which I believe will in A
month More, May rent at £200 per Annum the two Apartments
—My days have bin Many thro' God's Mercy, by Corse of Nature
Can not be Many More, My Son and Daughter to me are boath
alike, and think am bound in Duty to God and them too, to Treat
them alike as Near as possible, and such is my Intention; if Gousse'
Scheme don'te overthrow all, You will I hope think I have done
the Duty of A parent or rather More if you will Judge Impartial
for should Gousse faile at this [?] May put it Out of my power
giving my Daughter and Children One shilling. What I am doing
No Creditor Can touch. and should I attempt any Further Settlement On Your Daughter May be Looked on as an intended fraud
and bring all my Creditors on my back at Once; and As it is I fear
shall be Oblige to Sell the Other spot to pay the Demands Gousse
has brought upon me—for without they are Content with the Interest a few Years longer it must be the Case, I have no Other
Estate but liable to the same Accident as the former. and a few
days Ago Some Mischevious person Attempted the like by Seting
fire to A Neighbours house I may Say in the Midst of Mine, thro'
God's Mercy and Early discovery was quenched. the House was
afire outside of the Roof plainly Shows no Accident but premidatid
Several Such Like Attempts have bin Made Since our Dreadfull
Fire of the 17th August 1769—God preserve us from the Like.
Amen, Your Anxiety, behoves All Parents and good Christians
and hope you will not be backward to Your Daughter and Babes,
half of your Benovilence would have bin of More Service to New
biginnings those that waite dead Mens shoes may go a long time
barefoot. your Estate is Certain our Building as uncertain as the
Wind, and by what have heard you have no Other incumbrance
upon your Estate than Your Self Lady Palmer and Grandson Who
is an Infant and cannot be Expensive Many Years Yett. Nor Your
Selves above your income that a mite may be Spared now and
then to your Only Living Daughter. and Her Son and daughter,
not that I wish you to bring Your Selves under the Same delimna
I have done, and beg your pardon for the freedom I have taken.
my reason I hope will Modrate your Anxiety as it May Convince

my Intention to supporte them Long as in my power with Justice to the World bisid—I came Naked to the World and to my Earth Shall return So. Hoping God. thro' Jesus Christ will receive my Soul. Compliments of the Family Attends you. Lady Palmer, and the Young Gentleman your grandSon, the Blessings of God be with you all Amen beg leave to Conclude and assure you my best Effections and remain Dear Sir

Your Loving Kinsman
Henry Bonnin

APPENDIX 2

Philadelphia January 15th 1771

Hon Sir

In pursuance of the sacred promise I made of being in time with a remittance, I now inclose you the first of a sett of Exchange payable in London, although drawn upon a House in Glasgow, which bill I am of opinion you had better give into the hands of Child Your banker, to receive and carry to your Credit as you may depend on its being punctually paid at the Expiration of thirty days from the date of acceptance, the invoices Messrs. Willing and Morris being Men of the first responsibility here, and assuring me thereof; if the bill I drew the fourth of December should upon sight of this letter be on the point of becoming due, I must pray you to pay it upon the strength of the inclosed bill, I would not lead you into an error, and as you cannot be supposed to be acquainted very well with negotiation, mention the circumstance of your submitting the whole to Child, as if upon your Own account; I am but within these few minutes ascertain'd of the time of the Packett's sailing, or rather this post reaching the Packett which is upon the point of setting out

I am with the most lively affection Lady Palmer and
Hon Sir

Your most Dutifull Son
G. Bonnin

APPENDIX 3

Philadelphia January 15th 1771
Dear Lady Palmer

I this day have the pleasure of sending forward to Sir
Charles, a bill of Exchange for £100 [?] payable in London at
thirty days sight; which I hope will arrive in time to answer that
I drew upon him for an equal sum at sixty days sight the fourth
of December last; I have Mentioned to Sir Charles, the propriety
of immediately sending this bill to Child to Negotiate, as upon his
own account, having it carried regularly to his credit when paid,
which he may be assured will be punctual, as I purchase the bill
upon the word of the Endorsers' Messrs. Willing and Morris who
are men of the first responsibility in the Mercantile way here;
under these circumstances I flatter myself Sir Charles will find no
difficulty in paying off my bill, even should it be requisite before
this becomes due, and if in the negotiation he is brought into expenses that I am not aware of, he will please to deduct it out of
the thirty pounds he will receive upon my account by the way of
the West Indies, perhaps even before this letter reaches You

I think I can now congratulate myself on the flourishing posture
of our affairs, The China Factory is brought to a crisis and the first
Emission of ware which took place the 24th of December was
immediately bought up and most generally admired, I shall send
forth another large quantity in ten days, which is already bespoke,
nevertheless you may believe there are some faults in it, since no
work was ever suddenly [erased] immediately brought to perfection, but I shall pass no comments of my own, designing myself
the favour of presenting you with A sample by the first ship which
sails directly from this port to London. Our Toddy and the little
Tods are in full health we all Join in the most affectionate and
sincere professions of Unalterable Duty and Love and remain

My Dearest Mother   Your Obedient Son   G. Bonnin

The Inclosed is the second bill of the sett, whereof first is sent
forward to Sir Charles, that you receive soonest, please to negotiate
Directly, as either are of Equal force with the other.

APPENDIX 4

Philadelphia November 9th 1771

Dear Mother

He was a wise man who wept at the follies of mankind, but a much wiser one, who laugh'd at them; impressed with a full conviction of this truth, tho neither a Sage, or a Philosopher, I frequently smile at the wide diffrence, between my former and present pursuits in life, as also at the futile presages of those, who confidently foretold the impracticability, of my ever becoming a proficient in industry, and application, to business. That this is a strange world, is the repeated acknowledgment of every age, perhaps you'll say my Amendment is as strange, but remember *there is nothing new under the sun.* wether this adage, is to be taken in a literal sense, is not to the point in question, however you may rest assured, the lively sun of Gallantry and Jollity is set with me, and gives place, to the Calmer light of unremitted assiduity, in the furtherance of the China Manufactory. You request in your letter of July the 12th per *Falconer*, the particulars of this Manufactory, and how it is likely to succeed; a chearfull compliance with every request of yours, and Sir Charles's, is an actual gratification of my own pride, for proud I truely am, to be able, to contribute the least atom, towards your mutual tranquility or amusement.

I am a constant attendant upon the business of China making, and as it is a work of Critical nicety, and most extensive advantage, if rightly managed and understood; I suffer the Crucibles to lie dormant, until the first is brought so far forward, as to require less of my personal attendance, besides, this is no Country to Assert the priviledges of A Patent, without which the Crucibles could not be momentous, as the fabrication, when once begun, is so extremely open, and simple, as to render it impossible to be preserved a secret. if ever it is my fate to reside in Great Britain, there they will shine with proper lustre, duely supported by the Authority of the King, not so here. to return to the China work, I have the highest expectation of its being great in the extreme; people cease to stigmatize me for madness and folly in the undertaking; those who profess themselves my friends, applaud my *sagacious* perseverance; others with envy, cannot conceal thier distracted astonishment; My Father, struck with the pleasurable delight of my industry, and the prospect of my becoming usefull in my generation (I mean in the advancement of my Childrens' happiness and Fortunes), expresses more satisfaction to others, than he chooses to do in his letters to me. he has been extremely liberal in his pecuniary advances, much more so, than I could have flatterd myself; at first indeed, he was dubious, it was a stupendous undertaking, fraught with uncertainties, no body could unravel the mysterious system, and the Sanguine relations, of A Young man, were not entirely to be depended upon; his Wisdom is the product of Age, and his prudence the result of many years Experience; neither are to be treated lightly, far be it from me then, to do so; I reverence the man, and most affectionately adore the Father, in him. *Falconer* sails much sooner than I expected, or should have furnished you with a sample of my Porcelane; I shall however embrace the next safe opportunity; The Lottery I mentioned to you some time since, instituted by our friends, is not yet drawn; you are interested in some ticketts in partnership with myself, I sincerely wish you a good account of them, a faithfull one you may depend on as soon as drawn. Toddy writes, to her, I leave the family concerns, reserving to myself the presentation of my unfeigned duty to Sir Charles, and affectionate assurances of my remaining

Dear Mother
Your most Dutifull and Obliged Son
G. Bonnin

APPENDIX 5

Pennsylvania Chronicle
October 9, 1769
To the PUBLIC

WHEREAS it has pleased his Majesty, agreeable to a statute in that case provided, to grant his royal LETTERS PATENT, bearing date the fifth day of May last past, for the sole manufacturing and vending a certain kind of Crucibles known by the name of BLACK-LEAD Crucibles, for the term of 14 years, from the date of the said patent, within that part of his Majesty's kingdom of Great-Britain called England, his principality of Wales and town of Berwick upon Tweed; also, within all his Majesty's colonies and plantations abroad. In consequence whereof, the patentee is arrived from London; and forthwith intends to establish a manufactory of the said BLACK LEAD crucibles, which he doubts not will prove advantageous to the trade of the colonies in general, and of this province in particular. He is therefore inclinable to treat with any persons having blacklead to dispose of, and will handsomely reward all persons whatever, giving him intelligence of any offering to manufacture such crucibles, in contempt of these his Majesty's LETTERS PATENT. Applications to G. BONNIN, at his house in Water-street, near Messrs. Willing and Morris's store, will be attended to.

APPENDIX 6

January 30, 1771

An Address from the Proprietors of the China Manufactory, lately erected in this District of *Southwark*, was presented to the House, read, and follows in these Words, *viz.*

To the Honourable the REPRESENTATIVES *of the* FREEMEN *of the Province of* Pennsylvania, *in* GENERAL ASSEMBLY *now sitting.*

The ADDRESS *of the* Proprietors *of the* CHINA MANUFACTORY.

WORTHY SIRS,

WE the Subscribers, actuated as strongly by the sincerest Attachment to the Interest of the Public as to our private Emolument, have at our sole Risque and Expence introduced into this Province a Manufacture of Porcelain or China Earthen Ware, a Commodity, which, by Beauty and Excellence, hath forced its Way into every refined Part of the Globe, and created various imitative Attempts, in its Progress through the different Kingdoms and

Principalities of *Europe*, under the Sanction and Encouragement of their several Potentates. *Great-Britain*, which hath not been the least backward in Royal Testimonials of Favour to the first Adventurers in so capital an Undertaking, cannot yet boast of any great Superiority in Workmanship, surpassing *Denmark*, *France* and the *Austrian Netherlands*, she yields the Palm to *Saxony*, which in her Turn gives Place to the *East-Indies*. *America*, in this general Struggle, hath hitherto been unthought of, and it is our peculiar Happiness to have been primarily instrumental in bringing her forward; but how far she shall proceed, in a great Measure depends on the Influence of your generous Support. We have expended great Sums in bringing from *London* Workmen of acknowledged Abilities, have established them there, erected spacious Buildings, Mills, Kilns, and various Requisites, and brought the Work, we flatter ourselves, into no contemptible Train of Perfection. A Sample of it we respectfully submit to the Inspection of your Honourable House, praying it may be viewed with a favourable Eye, having Reference to the Disadvantages under which we engaged; if happy enough to merit your Approbation, we would not wish to aspire at the Presumption of dictating the Measure of your Encouragement, but with all Humility hint at the Manner. You, Gentlemen, who are appointed to a dignified Pre-eminence by the free Votes of your Countrymen, as well for your known Attachment to their truest Welfare, as superior Knowledge, must be sensible, that capital Works are not to be carried on by inconsiderable Aids or Advancements: Hence it is, we beg Leave to point out the Propriety of a Provincial Loan, at the Discretion of your Honourable House, independent of Interest, for a certain Term of Years. Under such Indulgence, on our Part, we shall not be deficient in the Display of a lively Gratitude, and the Promotion of the Colony's service, by the introducing of an additional Number of experienced Workmen, the Extension of our Buildings, and Improvement of the Manufacture, endeavouring to render it equal in Quality to such as is usually imported, and vending it at a cheaper Rate. We have the Honour to be, with the most profound Respect,

Worthy Sirs,   *Your obedient Servants,*

                                            GOUSSE BONNIN,
Philadelphia, January 22, 1771.   GEO. ANTH. MORRIS.

APPENDIX 7

Phila'd May the 10th 1771.

Mr Thomas Wharton

Bought of Arch. McElroy, American China

March the 19.	One Dozen of handled Cups etc.		£ 1 . 4.0
	Two Shugar Dishes	@6	12.0
	Two Cream Ewers	5	10.0
	Two teapots	7/6	15.0
	One Do	@6	6.0
	Foure Bowls	@2/6	10.0
March the 30.			
	T[w]o three pounds of tea	@ £1.7	4 . 1.0
May the 9.	One Shugar dish		3.0
	One pickle stand		15.0
	one fruit Basket		10.0
	13 plates	@1	13.0
	One Sett of Quitted Cups etc.		12.0
	One pair Sauce Boats		7.6
	One Sett of plain Cups		6.0
	One small Sauce boat		1.0
	Six pint Bowls		10.6
			£ 11.16.0

Pennsylvania Magazine, XXXIII (1909), 253.

John Cadwalader bt. of Arch. McElroy ... 1770   paid Jany. 1771

Two picklestands	@ 15s.	£ 1 . 10	
Foure fruit Baskets	@ 10s.	2 .	
Two Pair of Sauce boats		1 . 10	[or 1 . 0 .]
Four pint bowls	@ 2/6	10	
Six plate	@ 3s.	18	
Fifteen Large path [?] pans @ 1/8		1 . 5	
Ten small Do.	@ 1/6	15	
Two small sauce Boats		5	
		£ 8 . 3.0	

Cadwalader Collection, Historical Society of Pennsylvania.

APPENDIX 8

Pennsylvania Gazette
August 1, 1771
To the PUBLIC

PHILADELPHIA, August 1.

Every Inhabitant of *Pennsylvania* must observe, with Pleasure, the Progress we make in this Province towards Perfection in useful Arts, and the general Encouragement that is given to Genius and Industry by all Ranks of Men. It will be recorded, to the Honour of *Pennsylvania*, that an infant Colony, scarcely risen One Hundred Years from the rude Vestiges of Nature, has produced Men who shine in the learned and polite Arts amongst the first Characters of the present Age. The World is already indebted to this Province for one of the most useful mathematical Instruments that has ever been invented; for the most curious Piece of astronomical Mechanism, and for Discoveries in Natural Philosophy of singular Importance to Mankind. It would not be very easy to fix on the particular Soil or Climate, which is best fitted by Nature for the Cultivation of liberal Arts; but it will never be disputed that Liberty, in every Region, is the genuine Parent of Industry and Learning; under her Wings they are always found to thrive. In all Probability the rapid Progress of Arts in this Province, should be attributed to the salutary Influence of our Laws, and the perfect Liberty which we enjoy, rather than to any accidental Concurrence of favourable Incidents. The Friends of Liberty are ever found to be the first Persons who promote Works of Genius by their Countenance and Fortunes. No Affront can be intended to any particular Province, when it is remarked that the Assembly of *Pennsylvania* was the only public Body on the Continent, that, on a late Occasion, expended a considerable Sum of Money in making astronomical Observations, which, we are told, for their Accuracy and Perfection, would have done Credit to any State in *Europe*. The genteel Encouragement they have since given to a rising Genius for his elegant Piece of philosophical Mechanism, is another Proof of their Determination to support the growing Reputation of this Province. It is sincerely to be lamented, that the mechanic Arts and Manufactures cannot be encouraged by our Legislature with the same Propriety that they promote the liberal Arts and Sciences; but it happens some how, that our Mother Country apprehends she has a Right to manufacture every Article we consume, except Bread and Meat; our very Drink is to come through her Hands, or pay to her Support; in these Circumstances it cannot be doubted, that she would take great and insuperable Offence, at any Colony Legislature that should attempt to encourage domestic Manufactures; the smallest Proof of her Resentment that might be expected is, that she would disable them, as she did the New-York Assembly, on a different Occasion, from doing any Business, till they had reversed that Vote; were it not for this Impediment, we might expect to see the mechanic Arts soon arrive at great Perfection in this Province; they have already made a very promising Appearance; several Persons have been found willing to risque their Fortunes on the Event, and the Public, in general, has shewn a Desire to promote their Undertakings. Every Person seems pleased with the late Success of Mr. *Stiegel*, who has erected the first House in *America* for making White Flint Glass. We have already seen that Work brought to Perfection; Decanters, Wine Glasses, etc. are now manufactured in this Province, equal in Whiteness, Transparency and Figure, to those which are imported from *Europe*; that many Thousands of Pounds must be saved to *Pennsylvania* by this Manufacture alone, will readily be granted. When we consider the extensive Consumption of Glass, and the great Price of that Commodity, it will hardly be disputed that a Man has some Claim to a public Reward, who had the Spirit and Fortitude to risque his Estate in erecting such a Manufacture, by which the Province will presently save Twenty or Thirty Thousand Pounds *per Annum*. Another Manufacture has been erected, of similar Importance to the Public, though we are told, that the Work is more curious, more hazardous, and much more expensive. Glass has long been manufactured in *Great-Britain* and *Ireland*, in the utmost Perfection, but China Ware is the Production of a foreign Country, which the *English* have only attempted to imitate within these few Years. It has been observed, as characteristic of the *English*

Nation, that they take up the Inventions of other People, and generally bring them to greater Perfection than the Inventors were able to do; how far this may hold good in the Article of China, must be reserved to the Decision of Time; but from the Progress they have made, they bid fair to overtake their Originals in a few Years, if the Factories, Labourers and all, should not be swallowed up in the Vortex of an *East-India* Company.

The Manufacture of China Ware in this Province, certainly deserves the serious Attention of every Man, who prays for the Happiness of his Fellow-subjects, or that the very Semblance of Liberty may be handed down to Posterity. I would not be mistaken on this Subject; I would not have it supposed, that Happiness is naturally connected with China Ware, or even with Tea, its general Attendant; I sincerely wish they were both, with all their concomitant Plagues, in the Bottom of the Red-sea; but we must consider Matters as they are, and try to make the best of them, rather than hope for a perfect Revolution. The Use of China is introduced, and well established; Custom has rendered it some how necessary; we must and will have it, whatever be the Consequence. No less than Fifteen Thousand Pounds Worth of China has been imported into this Province since the first of *April* last; if this Clay be paid for, there are Fifteen Thousand Pounds of Gold and Silver less in the Province than we should have had, if the same Ware had not been imported, but manufactured amongst us; add to this annually, the immense Sums that are sent away for every Species of Dry Goods, etc. and the Amount will be very alarming. No Man of common Sense will venture to say, that the Province can long endure such enormous Taxes. Every Thing that is alienable must soon change its Owner; the Property will be transferred to the other Side the *Atlantic*. We must certainly investigate some Method of saving Cash; we must manufacture some Things for ourselves; no Manufactures are so ill fitted for Exportation as Glass and China; none can be made with more Propriety at Home. These we should make, and many Things besides, else we shall soon be a ruined People. Our Mother Country has left no Measures untried, which may crush our Manufactures, check the Spirit of Patriotism, and keep us in the Chains of Subjection: *Obsia Principiis*, is her Maxim; she would nip us in the Bud. The China Manufactory has supplied us with a cogent Proof of this melancholy Fact. Every Importer of China knows, and most retail Purchasers have observed with Pleasure, that the Price of China is fallen Five Shillings in the Pound, since the Commencement of a China Factory in this Place; the natural Consequence of this Change should be a full Stop to the *American* Manufactory, and a full Stop it must have made, had not the Spirit of Liberty taken a just Alarm at this insidious Scheme. Few Men of large Fortunes engage in new Enterprizes. These are commonly left to the young Adventurer, who has not so much to lose. Such Persons often, at the Expence of all they possess, lay the Foundation for Improvements, which become a national Advantage; they are sure of being praised by Posterity, but have frequently the Fate of being deserted by their Cotemporaries. We are apt to discourage new Inventions and home Manufactures, because they are not quite so cheap, or not yet quite so good, as antient or foreign Ones. A Neighbour of mine, who was rocked in the very Cradle of Despotism, is become such a Patriot as to declare, that he should prefer Home Manufactures to Foreign, provided they were equal in Quality and Price; until that Time, he counts it his Duty to buy at the cheapest Shop. This Man often puts me in Mind of a certain Islander, who could never consent that his Son should go into the Water, 'til he had learned to swim; if we do not encourage imperfect Works, we shall never get perfect Ones. Little do such Persons consider, that by purchasing pretty and cheap foreign Manufactures, we shall, in a little Time, have nothing left wherewith to buy Goods of any Kind. I should not commend the Propriety and Virtue of supporting the Manufacture in Question, through the contracted View of saving Twenty or Thirty Thousand Pounds *per Annum*. This very Manufacture may soon become the Means of saving the Sum of Two or Three Hundred Thousand Pounds *per Annum* to ourselves and our Neighbours. The Success of one Adventurer never fails to give Motion and Spirit to a Number, and the Miscarriage of a single Person in a new Enterprize, has often damped the public Ardour for a Series of Years. The *East-India* Company would avail themselves of these Foibles of Humanity; if they could demolish one noted Manufacture, they would certainly clip twenty Years from the Growth of *American* Improvements, and what they lost in the present and following Year, by lowering their Prices, they would gain in succeeding Years, with sufficient Interest: We should then wish we had a Factory in the Neighbourhood, where we might, like the

Egyptians, when our Money was all gone, be able to procure the necessary Articles in Barter, for our Produce or other Effects; but we should wish in vain. One House demolished in a fruitless Enterprize, would be set up as a Land-mark to admonish the cautious Passenger to stand clear of *American* Manufactures, and we should sail on secure in the antient Channel, 'til, deprived of every Thing that is desirable to rational Beings, we sunk down into the most wretched State of Indigence and Servitude. When I consider the plausible Attempt that has been made to lead us aside from our true Interest, under the Colour of consulting our Profit and Pleasure, and when I observe the general Efforts that are made, notwithstanding of these Schemes, to support the Spirit of useful Improvements in this Province, I cannot help congratulating myself, that I was born in a Colony, which will, in all Probability, be the best Retreat of Liberty.

A PENNSYLVANIA PLANTER.

APPENDIX 9

Pennsylvania Journal
November 11, 1772
To the Printers of the *Pennsylvania Journal*

The feelings of a benevolent heart instruct us, not only to compassionate the distresses of our fellow creatures, but to pity and extend our generosity even to their faults; since the most humane and thoughtful of mankind are frequently, by accident or through passion, betrayed into unworthy actions. What then shall be said of a late advertiser, who has ungenerously and disingenuously attempted to check the rising benevolence of the public, towards some unhappy people, whose misfortunes are really not owing to their own, but the faults of others. It is a subject so generally known, that perhaps it may be needless to say, the author of an advertisement in the Pennsylvania Gazette, dated Southwark, Nov. 2, 1772, is here meant.

The faults of these poor people, if any, while they have been in this country, I will not endeavour to excuse; but can say, that they were only such common errors as Europeans generally fall into at their first arrival here; and did, by no means, contribute to the failure of the late China Manufactory of this city, consequently, their application for relief, could not excite the resentment of the directors; surely therefore it is cruel, very cruel, to oppose the good intentions of the public, since their case will appear truly pitiable.

I make no reflections to the disadvantage of any one; unknowing and unknown, I question not the integrity of any person; nor can I deny that the Proprietors of the late China Work, tho' unsuccessful, are entitled to praise for their endeavours to introduce so valuable a Manufactory: But they should recollect that the present misfortunes of the poor workmen are altogether owing to want of judgment, or proper information previous to these endeavours, in the Managers; and if they cannot fulfil the first engagement they entered into, which, from the pleasing prospect it afforded, drew these people from an easy situation in life; they ought, at least, to do what they *can*, to restore them to that situation; and I am persuaded, the public will agree with me when they are told, That, the workmen, who were lately engaged in the China Manufactory of this city, when first applied to in England, were in easy and comfortable circumstances; esteemed as artificers, respected as men: but allured by the very tempting offers of the conductors of that work, they quitted their native country; separated themselves from agreeable connexions, and left a certain competence of fortune for their condition, for an uncertain, tho' promised, abundance; induced thereto, by the following agreement, made and fully confirmed by the Proprietors of the said China Work, viz.

The said Proprietors agreed to pay their passage to America, and for five years after a weekly salary of One Guinea and an Half; in consideration of their doing such work as the said Proprietors should have occasion for, twelve hours in the day, allowing two hours for the time of meals; and for any part of the remaining ten hours, which the workmen should waste, a due proportion of said salary was to be deducted. The Proprietors, on their part, have exacted a full obedience from the men to this agreement, even so far as frequently to deduct for a quarter of an hour, in which a workman has attended the call of an occasional acquaintance; but they have not so scrupulously fulfilled their own engagement; and this failure, whatever the cause, has reduced these unhappy people from a comfortable enjoyment of life to the want of its necessaries, some being advanced in years, and all unable to turn their hands to any other employment, in a distant country, where they are strangers and friendless: Yet they have not, as the advertiser would insinuate, meanly gone begging about, and uttering their reproaches against the Proprietors of the late Manufactory, but modestly wish and desire only, though they suppose they might insist upon a performance of articles, since they cannot support themselves by any means in this country, to be restored to their own, where they can still live in plenty by their honest endeavours.

This, I doubt not, the candid will think, the Proprietors owe to justice and to the community, for though they too have been sufferers in the common misfortune, they have not, as is the case of these poor people, lost their *All*; but are still very able to make some amends, by sending them back to their former easy situation; and by restoring to society a number of very useful members.

APPENDIX 10

Pennsylvania Chronicle
December 12, 1772

Philadelphia, December 11, 1772.
An alteration in the late advertisement being necessary, for the better accommodation of purchasers, and the Acting Proprietor under a necessity of embarking with his family for England, on board of one of the first spring ships, without the least prospect of ever returning to this continent, Public Notice is hereby given, that the China Manufactory will be peremptorily sold by Auction to the highest bidder, at the London Coffee-House, between the hours of five and eight, on Monday evening, the 21st inst. in two separate Lots, the first to consist of a building three stories high, besides garret, 80 feet in length, and 15 in depth, situate on Prime street, with ground of equal breadth, extending 100 feet back, to a new street, 32 feet wide, purposely laid out and called China street, in

which is an excellent new pump, for the general use of the contiguous lots; this building with little expence may be converted into four habitable tenements; the second lot, to consist of sundry strong and spacious buildings, containing three kilns, two furnaces, two mills, two clay vaults, cisterns, engines, and treading room, of the utmost utility to any person inclinable to enter upon the China or Potting business, in either of their most extensive branches; with little expence may be extremely suitable for a Glass House, or small work, or sundry mechanical branches. On Tuesday the 22d, between the hours of one and four in the afternoon, will also be exposed to public sale, on the premises, sundry lots of ground situate on Front and Prime Streets, adjoining the manufactory; some of which are well improved. A plan of the whole to be seen at the London Coffee House. And, on Wednesday the 23d, between the same hours, in the China House Yard, will be exposed to public sale, in various lots, all the moulds, models, laths, and wheels, together with a great quantity of painted and plain unglazed China Ware, two hand mills for grinding clay; also a Potter's mill, with several other matters too tedious for an advertisement. The whole may be viewed every day until the sale, and terms made known, by applying at the China House, and an undisputable title, and immediate possession, if required, will be given.

APPENDIX 11

Pennsylvania Journal
August 3, 1774

China Manufactory.
Office for the Sale of Real Estates.
This day, at three o'clock in the afternoon, will be sold by public vendue, at the late China Factory, in the District of Southwark, a pair of large mill-stones, each stone surrounded with a circle of cast iron, weighing about two tons and an half, and run on a circular cast iron plate of the same weight: Also a wrought iron axis, and a large shaft on which they run. The stones are fixed in

the manner of a Tanner's bark-mill, for which purpose they would be very useful.

Sundry iron-bolts, gudgeons, screws and burs of various sizes.

Pieces of bar-iron and iron-works of different sizes.

A shaft and frame-work of a large mill, which is surrounded by a cedar frame of set work, hooped with iron; the inside is paved with very smooth large flat stone, which will be sold in such manner as will best suit the purchasers. They are very proper to grind paint upon.

Sundry large tubs and vats of various shapes and sizes, very suitable for soap-boilers, etc.

Two iron stoves, with their pipes.

A rolling press, for copper-plate printing; and other articles made use of in the China Factory.

Some of the buildings, and ground on which they stand, are to be let on ground rent, by

Matthew Clarkson,
Edward Bonsall.

Alfred Coxe Prime, comp., *The Arts and Crafts in Philadelphia, Maryland and South Carolina, 1721–1785* (Topsfield, Mass., 1929), 123.

APPENDIX 12

Whilst these fruitless attempts were making in Carolina, another equally fruitless, and equally fatal to our people (for *they* were chiefly employed in it) was carried on in Pennsylvania. Here a sort of China ware was aimed at, and eight men went over at first; whether any more, or how many, might follow, I have not learnt. The event was nearly the same in this as in the others; the proprietors, soon finding that they had no chance of succeeding, not only gave up the undertaking, but silenced the just complaints of the poor injured workmen, by clapping one of them (Thomas Gale) into a prison: the rest who had never received half the wages agreed for, were left entirely to shift for themselves. Thus abandoned, at the distance of some thousands of miles from home, and without a penny in their pockets, they were reduced to the hard necessity of begging in the public streets for a morsel of bread. Some died immediately, of sickness occasioned by this great change in their prospects and manner of living, being dashed at once from the highest expectations to the lowest and most abject misery. Mr. Byerley a nephew of mine, who was then upon the spot, published in the newspapers, a letter in behalf of the poor survivors, stating the original agreement upon which they had been brought over, the injustice and cruelty of their employers, and the miserable circumstances to which the men were reduced. This had no effect in softening the hearts of their masters towards them, but a subscription was set on foot by the inhabitants for their relief, by which those who had weathered the first storm were supplied with daily bread; but, like plants removed into a soil unnatural to them, they dwindled away and died, and not one was left alive, to return and give us any farther particulars of this affecting tale.

Josiah Wedgwood, *An Address to the Workmen in the Pottery: On the Subject of Entering into the Service of Foreign Manufacturers* (Newcastle, Staffordshire, 1783), 8–9.

APPENDIX 13

LOT PROVENIENCE SUMMARY

Stratigraphic Definition	*Areal Definition*			
	ON/OW	ON/6W	6N/OW	2S/6W
20th Century				
Leaf mold, shed floor, addition floor, concrete, etc.	19, 22	2	39, 41	32
Pipe trench after 1940		4	42	
Postholes	16	5, 6		33, 35
Animal burrows	18, 30	3		

Stratigraphic Definition	ON/OW	Areal Definition ON/6W	6N/OW	2S/6W
Late 19th Century				
Brick yard paving	17	7	40	
Occupation level beneath paving	20, 23, 24			
Early brickbat privy paving	21			
Privy construction ditch backfill	25			
Circa 1775–1860				
Dark brown sandy loam				
top half	26	8	43	34
bottom half	26	9	44	34
1780s				
Detritis fill above privy			47	
Circa 1774–1780				
Refuse fill top of privy			49	
Privy fill			50	
1769–1772				
Sagger stratum	29	10	45	36
Small pockets of factory debris worked into brown sandy loam		11	46	
Construction spoil below saggers		12		
Kiln waste below construction spoil		13		
Pre-1769				
Brown sandy loam				
top half	31	14	48	37
bottom half	31	15	48	37

APPENDIX 14

SHARD COUNT

Underglaze red	3	Plate	
saucer footrings (2)		rims	3 (1–8½″)
punch bowl footring (1)		footrings—4¹³⁄₃₂″	6
Transfer-Printed	4+	Untypable	
		thin rims	48
Sauceboats		thick rims	7
scalloped rims	2	small footrings	20
molded dots	1	body—decorated	50
scalloped, banded,		glazed only	33
dotted	1	bisque or unfired	
floral molding	19	over ⅛″	
rims—plain	1	thickness	48
body shards—plain	2	under ⅛″	
		thickness	336
Punch bowl		misc. molded shards	10
rim, footring,		Pierced fruit basket	
body shards	16	lattice and molded	
		flowers	4
Cup			
rims—3½″	13	Handles	
footrings—1¹¹⁄₃₂″	9	oval cross section	3
footring—1½″	1	round cross section	6
Saucer		Fluted pieces	7
rims—5¼″	15		
footrings—3¼″	16	Centerpiece (?) stem,	
footrings—3″	24	horizontally banded	1
Bowl—small		Crucible bases	2
rims—4½″	15		
(?) footring—2²³⁄₃₂″	1	"Quilted" ware	
		cup	6
Bowl—medium		saucer	1
body shards	4	sauceboat	1
		punch bowl	1
		bowl	1
		misc. body shards	10

APPENDIX 15

SIZES OF SAGGERS

PINK CLAY SAGGERS

Diameter	*Height*
8 ½"	over 2½"
9 ¾"	over 3"
10 "	2¼"
10 "	3"
10 "	3¼"
10 "	over 4½"
12 "	4½"
13 "	2"
13 "	2¾"
13 "	2⅞"
13 "	3⅛"
13 "	3¼"
13 "	4½"
13 "	5⅜"
13 "	over 8"
14 ½"	over 5¼"

YELLOW CLAY SAGGERS

Diameter	*Height*
8 ½"	4¼"
9 ¼"	?
10 "	3⅞"
12 "	over 3¼"
13 "	3½"
14 ½"	?

Notes

———————◆•◆———————

1. The earliest historical mention of the Bonnin and Morris factory is found in Dr. James Mease, *Picture of Philadelphia* (Philadelphia, 1811), 75. Essentially the same information is repeated in John F. Watson, *Annals of Philadelphia* (Philadelphia, 1844), II, 272: "A china factory too was also erected on Prime Street, near the present Navy Yard, intended to make china at a saving of £15,000." A footnote indicates the following: "This long row of wooden houses afterwards became famous as a sailor's brothel and riot house on a large scale. The former frail ware proved an abortive scheme." This information was repeated by almost all subsequent Philadelphia historians. See also E. A. Barber, *The Pottery and Porcelain of the United States* (New York, 1893), 91–100.
2. *Early American Pottery and China* (New York, 1926), 76–84.
3. *American Potters and Pottery* (Boston, 1939), 45, 98–100.
4. *Our Pioneer Potters* (New York, 1947), 60–65.
5. "Found! Bonnin and Morris Porcelain," *Antiques*, LIX (1951), 139. This classification of the wares as "glazed earthenware" is still common; see Louis B. Wright *et al.*, eds., *The Arts in America: The Colonial Period* (New York, 1966), 333.
6. The Tucker factory actually produced hard-paste porcelain (hardly a novelty in 1830), but it has always been claimed as the first factory in America to make any kind of porcelain in any quantity.

7. Carl Bridenbaugh, *Cities in Revolt: Urban Life in America, 1743–1776* (New York, 1971), 217*n*, modifies his earlier statement that in the 1770s Philadelphia was the second largest city in the British Empire. Sam Bass Warner, Jr., in his *The Private City: Philadelphia in Three Periods of Its Growth* (Philadelphia, 1968), chap. 1, calculates that the population of the city in 1775 was only about 24,000, which, according to Bridenbaugh's figures, would have made it the sixth and possibly even the seventh largest city in the empire.
8. "A Variety of Bow China, Cups and Saucers, Bowls, etc. . . . just imported by Philip Breadnig, and to be sold at his House in Fish Street." *Boston Evening Post*,

Nov. 11, 1754, G. F. Dow, *The Arts and Crafts in New England, 1704–1775* (Topsfield, Mass., 1927), 88. From the same source it can be seen that china figurines were also available in America: "A variety of curious fine China in Statuary: also some of the best enamel'd China, sold at public auction at the House next to the Orange Tree in Hanover Street." *Boston Gazette*, May 17, 1762, quoted *ibid.*, 90.

9. R. C. Moon, *The Morris Family of Philadelphia* (Philadelphia, 1898), 276, 489. A letter from Joseph Morris to Anthony Shoemaker, May 11, 1772, speaks of "George being in Carolina." Morris Papers, Historical Society of Pennsylvania, Philadelphia. Notice of Morris's death was given in the *Pennsylvania Gazette* (Philadelphia), Nov. 17, 1773. Morris was not the only one to provide influential contacts for the factory in Philadelphia, however; Bonnin, an old Etonian, would probably have known other Etonians in Philadelphia such as Richard Penn, lieutenant governor of the province from 1771 to 1773.

10. The indenture is in the Cadwalader Collection, Book D, IV, 207, Hist. Soc. Pa. For many of the details of Bonnin's life I am indebted to Col. Palmer; in the absence of a specific footnote, Col. Palmer is the authority for any factual statement relating directly to Bonnin's life.

11. In Oct. 1769 they were living on Water Street (see App. 5), and by June 1770 they had moved to George Street, between Cedar and Shippen, in the district of Southwark. *Philadelphia Contributionship Survey Book 1*, June 26, 1770.

12. *Chronological Index of Patents of Invention* (London, 1854), 165, no. 919. The Index refers to Letters Patent of Mar. 5, 1769, but the specification, signed by Bonnin on July 25, refers to the Letters Patent of May 5, 1769. The complete charge for the application and issuance of a patent at that time was about £60.

13. Only three days before Bonnin announced his crucible patent in Philadelphia (see App. 5), the American Philosophical Society, meeting of Oct. 6, 1769, agreed upon a motion "to publish an advertisement for specimens of the different clays to be sent to this society." This may have been prompted by, or against, Bonnin. At the society's meeting of Nov. 3, 1769, it was agreed to defer for some time the publication of any such advertisement. The development from the production of a highly fired ceramic crucible for commercial uses to the manufacture of porcelain for a primarily domestic market is explored more fully in Cyril Staal, "Calenick Crucibles," *124 Annual Report of the Royal Cornwall Polytechnic Society* (Falmouth, 1957), 44–54. It may be that Bonnin did plan to develop the crucible manufacture separately; in the 1773 tax lists for Southwark is the name of "Thomas Jackson, potter" who appears to have lived near Bonnin and who advertised "Black Lead Crucibles, made in Philadelphia and much better than any imported" (*Pa. Gaz.* [Phila.], Jan. 5, 1774).

14. The first land transaction is recorded in Philadelphia City Hall, Deed Book, I, 9, 50–53; the second is in Deed Book, I, 9, 54–57.

15. All the newspaper advertisements pertaining to the factory are given in full in Alfred Coxe Prime, comp., *The Arts and Crafts in Philadelphia, Maryland and South Carolina, 1721–1785* (Topsfield, Mass., 1929), 114–124. Prime does not indicate that almost all of them appeared in more than one newspaper, more than once; they are not quoted in full here.

16. The mention in this advertisement of Bow and "the clays of America" in the same breath immediately gives rise to speculation about the possible role of Andrew Duché in this enterprise. Duché, who was in Philadelphia about this time, has been named as an entrepreneur previously shipping clays from South Carolina to London for the use of the Bow factory; however, there is no known connection between him and Bonnin and Morris, nor is there any evidence that clays were ever shipped from America to England in any quantity. See Graham Hood, "The Career of Andrew Duché," *Art Quarterly*, XXXI (1968), 168–184.

17. This letter, to be quoted in full later, is now in the archives of the Philadelphia Museum of Art.

18. "A Memoir of Thomas Gilpin," *Pennsylvania Magazine of History and Biography*, XLIX (1925), 309–310.

19. In reference to this area Heinrich Ries, *Clays, Their Occurrence, Properties, and Uses, With Especial Reference to Those of the United States* (New York, 1906), 296, contains the single statement: "The Potomac beds of the coastal plain area are said to contain stoneware and fireclays, which have been dug at two localities not far from Wilmington." Neither the extensive state history by Henry C. Conrad, *The History of the State of Delaware* (Wilmington, 1908), II, 488–500, nor a more intimate account by Francis A. Cooch, *Little Known History of Newark, Delaware, and Its Environs* (Newark, 1936) makes any mention of clay mines among all the extensive references to gristmills, sawmills, etc., in the area.

20. The South Carolina advertisement is given in full in Prime, *Arts and Crafts in Philadelphia*, 115–116; Edward Lightwood, who was apparently acting as agent for Bonnin and Morris, was a successful merchant in Charleston (his will was probated Apr. 10, 1798; courtesy of E. Milby Burton). The Bonnin and Morris advertisement is dated several months before Bartlem's first recorded advertisement in the *South Carolina Gazette* (Charleston) of Oct. 4, 1770 (Prime, *Arts and Crafts in Philadelphia*, 112), which stated "A China Manufactory and Pottery is soon to be opened in this town (Charleston) . . . by Messrs. Bartlem and Company, the proper Hands, etc., for carrying it on having lately arrived here from England." Bartlem apparently left England between Jan. 1762 and the middle of the following year (Aqualate Hall Papers, D. 1788, p. 1 [1], D. 1788, v. 102, William Salt Library, Stafford; courtesy of John Mallet). He thus appears to have established a factory elsewhere in South Carolina between 1763 and 1770. This is confirmed in the famous letter from Josiah Wedgwood to his parliamentary patron, Sir William Meredith, Mar. 2, 1765: "This trade to our colonies we are apprehensive of loseing in a few years, as they have set on foot some Potworks there already, and have at this time an agent amongst us hireing a number of our hands for establishing new Pottworks in South Carolina, haveing got one of our insolvent Master Potters [Bartlem] there to conduct them, haveing material there equal, if not superior, to our own for carrying on the Manufactorie; and as the necessaries etc. of life and consequently the price of Labor amongst us are daily upon the advance, I make no question but more will follow them and join their Brother artists and Manufacturers of every class, who are from all quarters Takeing a rapid flight indeed the same way. . . . We cannot help apprehending such consequences from these emigrations as make us very uneasy for our trade and our Posterity." Ann Finer and George Savage, eds., *Selected Letters of Josiah Wedgwood* (London, 1965), 29. Wedgwood was concerned about losing the extremely profitable colonial trade not only because his own workers rejected his strict disciplinary control and were tempted by the higher wages offered by Bartlem but also because of his knowledge that the South Carolina clays were "equal, if not superior," to those available in England. Bow had experimented with these clays ("unaker") during 1744–1749, and Wedgwood himself conducted experiments with it at this time. Hood, "Career of Andrew Duché," *Art Qtly.*, XXXI (1968), 179. Bartlem, however, does not seem to have been able to use these clays with any degree of success: "Having opened his Pottery and China Manufactory . . . Will be much obliged to Gentlemen in the Country, or others, who will be so kind to send him samples of any Kinds of fine Clay upon their Plantations, etc., in order to make them Trials of. He already makes what is called Queen's Ware, equal to any imported." *S.C. Gaz.* (Charleston), Jan. 31, 1771; Prime, *Arts and Crafts in Philadelphia*, 112. As this is Bartlem's last recorded advertisement, Wedgwood need hardly have worried for his vast overseas trade.

His frame of mind, however, is reflected in the following quotation from William Chaffers, *Marks and Monograms on European and Oriental Pottery and Porcelain*, 14th ed. (London, 1932), pertaining to the Bonnin and Morris factory: "In January 1771, a paragraph states: 'The Philadelphians have established a china manufactory. In time they will serve North America and prevent the exportation of our English China.' " Bartlem was a subject upon which Wedgwood could become overheated with little effort. Twenty years later, in his *Address to the Workmen in the Pottery: On the Subject of Entering into the Service of Foreign Manufacturers* (Newcastle, Staffordshire, 1783), he vituperated against Bartlem at length, painting an idyllic picture of Staffordshire life, waxing rhetorical on the unmitigated horrors of life in America and waving the flag with great abandon (see App. 12). In this pamphlet Wedgwood mentioned three other workmen who migrated to South Carolina, "Mr. Lymer, Mr. Allen of Great Fenton and William Ellis of Hanley." The latter, who was the only one to return, found his way to Winston-Salem, N.C., where he helped the Moravians make queensware. James H. Craig, *The Arts and Crafts in North Carolina* (Winston-Salem, N.C., 1965), 88.

21. In November of the same year Bonnin was still promising to send a sample of his porcelain; whether or not he ever did is unknown. The Palmers were then living in a rented house in London; if they received a sample of Bonnin's porcelain there, it was not apparently taken to Dorney Court. In the same month as this first letter a notice appeared in the *Weekly Magazine or Edinburgh Amusement*, Jan. 17, 1771, 90: "By a letter from Philadelphia we are informed that a large china manufactory is established there, and that better china cups and saucers are made there than at Bow or Stratford."

22. The advertisements are given in full in Prime, *Arts and Crafts in Philadelphia*, 120–124.

23. Wedgwood never mentioned this factory by name, but there is no doubt that Bonnin and Morris were the culprits. Wedgwood mentioned eight workmen, while the newspaper announcement specified nine, but Wedgwood was writing ten years later. The phrase Wedgwood employed in this context—"our people (for *they* were chiefly employed in it)"—could mean either English rather than colonial workers or workers from Wedgwood's own factory. For example, when Wedgwood visited a small pottery in Bovey Tracy, Devon, in 1775, he wrote: "They afterwards made white stoneware, glazed with Salts, and had a fireman, and I believe some other workmen, from our country, but it was still a losing concern to them." Bernard Watney, "Engravings as the Origin of Designs and Decorations for English Eighteenth-Century Ceramics," *Burlington Magazine*, CVIII (1966), 406–410. However, there is no record of Thomas Gale in connection with Wedgwood, nor is there any record at Barlaston of any of the other potters whose names occur in connection with the site after the closing of the factory (courtesy of William Billington, Wedgwood Factory Records, Wedgwood Museum). These will be listed later. Of course, it is possible that Gale and the others were not master potters at all but rather skilled workmen. Even if the master workmen had not made porcelain at Wedgwood's factory, it is more than likely that they had migrated there from Derby, Worcester, or Bow, where they had made porcelain. N. McKendrick, "Josiah Wedgwood and Factory Discipline," *Proceedings of the Wedgwood Society*, no. 5 (1963), 1–29.

24. However, Mr. Byerley, a partner in the Wedgwood firm in the 1790s, informed Mr. Gilpin (see n. 18) that he was first employed in the Bonnin and Morris factory, "which was more of French than English origin."

25. Prime, *Arts and Crafts in Philadelphia*, 117. In Apr. 1770 Lord North repealed all duties except those on tea, thus competition from imported wares became increasingly severe.

26. The quotation is from an advertisement of Jan. 10, 1771, *ibid.*, 117, and the items described were billed to John Cadwalader (App. 7). Although American china is not mentioned on the bill, the prices are identical to that on the bill of Thomas Wharton (App. 7).

27. Carpenter Wharton's letter is in the *Papers of Sir William Johnson* (New York, 1933), VIII, 293–294 (courtesy of Milo Naeve and Lewis Rubenstein). The glass factory mentioned was Stiegel's. Archaeologists from the State of New York excavated the surrounds of Johnson Hall within recent years—the only wasters that the author was able to discover that might have had relevance to the Bonnin and Morris factory were too small to be useful.

28. The remainder of the reference to the factory in this letter is as follows: "In the meantime Jenny begs her Acceptance of a Sugar Dish as a specimen of the Philadelphia China, which I shall forward by the first opportunity with one of the same sort which she sends for my sister." Balch Collection, Hist. Soc. Pa. The use of zaffer is described in Bernard Watney, *English Blue and White Porcelain of the Eighteenth Century* (London, 1963), 6–9.

29. The partners persistently advertised for apprentices and for painters "either in blue or enamel." They seem to have built up a stockpile of bones by Apr. 1770—"notwithstanding their declining the reception of any more bones, they are determined to carry on the works upon the most extensive principles. . . ." Prime, *Arts and Crafts of Philadelphia*, 117. In May 1772 they advertised for "good Pot and Pearl Ashes" (pearl ash being refined potash) for use in the preparation of the glaze.

30. A ticket for the lottery was known to E. A. Barber, *Pottery and Porcelain*, 95; John Cadwalader paid £135 for 90 tickets in Nov. 1771, Cadwalader Coll., Hist. Soc. Pa.

31. Stiegel also had his hopes raised by the Nonimportation Agreement in 1769. In that year he built his second Manheim glass house, the "American Flint Glass Works," the first in America to produce glass presumably equal in quality and content to lead glass. He added to his factory each year for the next three years. But as early as 1770 he was in financial difficulties; in Sept. 1770 he too appealed for a provincial loan. A year later he was given the useless sum of £150. In 1773 he resorted to a lottery, and the following year he closed his factory. At its peak his factory employed 130 men, but Stiegel was only too conscious of the high cost of labor and the unbeatable competition of imported wares.

32. The style of this long letter bears a singular resemblance to Bonnin's, and the conclusion—an extended peroration on liberty, having previously run the gamut of self-sacrifice, decency, chauvinism, and amour propre—resembles Wedgwood's *Address to the Workmen*. Whoever the author was, he might have expressed perhaps justifiable resentment at the widespread local support given to the attempted culture of silk worms, when glass and porcelain factories were allowed to founder. The stress upon £15,000 worth of imported china between Apr. (when North repealed the duties) and Aug. 1771, and the need to keep such a large sum of money in the provinces, was probably the source for the previously quoted statement in Watson's *Annals* (see n. 1). I am grateful to Dr. James H. Hutson for drawing my attention to the larger implications of this letter.

33. No record of Bonnin's death has been found nor is there any will. In Aug. 1778 Bonnin's father died in Antigua; in Oct. 1780 Dorothy Bonnin opened an account with the Bank of England and was described as "Widow of Bristol." It is possible that Bonnin died at sea on the way to or from Antigua, where he may well have gone to attend his father's funeral or settle his estate. His widow found it necessary to seek her relatives' help in educating her five children. One of her sons returned to live and teach in Philadelphia.

34. As can be seen from figs. 20–21, the site of the factory was immediately divided into small lots. Apart from Thomas Jackson, the potter, already mentioned (see n. 13), two other potters later lived near the factory; Jonathan Carr (d. 1784), potter, is listed in the tax records (Philadelphia City Hall), for 1775 and 1779, and James Roberts is mentioned in the latter list as living next door to Carr. A piece of a large jar of brown, salt-glazed stoneware, bearing the incised mark "CARR & ROBERTS" (fig. 42) was found on the site of the factory. A part of the factory was used as a brass foundry for casting cannons during the Revolutionary War; John Adams wrote on Mar. 30, 1777: "I then went to the Foundry of Brass Cannon. It is in Front Street in Southwark, nearly opposite to the Sweedes Church. This Building was formerly a China Manufactory, but is now converted into a Foundery, under the Direction of Mr. Biers [Byers], late of New York." Lyman H. Butterfield, ed., *Adams Family Correspondence* (Cambridge, Mass., 1963), II, 190 (courtesy of Paul R. Huey). The main building of the factory, according to deeds and tax records, was "destroyed" about 1801. During the next 30 years or so the site was divided by another large road, and houses were extensively built upon it.

35. Nor was Chinese porcelain the only hard paste available in Philadelphia at the time. According to the inventory of his household, taken in 1788, John Penn, Jr., owned "a set of elegant Dresden tea china" comprising 63 pieces. *Pa. Mag. Hist. Biog.*, XV (1891), 374.

36. Finer and Savage, eds., *Letters of Wedgwood*, 28.

37. Wedgwood's two letters are in Eliza Meteyard, *The Life of Wedgwood: From His Private Correspondence and Family Papers* (London, 1865–1866), II, 56, 131–132. The Washington reference is in B. A. Born, "Josiah Wedgwood's Queens Ware," *Bulletin of the Metropolitan Museum of Art* (May 1964), 294.

38. The range of Worcester prices, ca. 1760, is given in Watney, *English Blue and White Porcelain*, 48–49; Wedgwood prices are in Wolf Mankowitz, *Wedgwood* (London, 1953), 63. A Hessian in Philadelphia (Capt. John Heinrichs) wrote in 1778: "A manufacture was established at Mannheim . . . but it thrives as poorly as the manufacture of china . . . because the price of labor is so high." *Pa. Mag. Hist. Biog.*, I (1875–1876), 43. Dr. James Mease noted: "Experiments show that ware equal to that of Staffordshire might be manufactured here, if WORKMEN COULD BE PROCURED." *Picture of Philadelphia*, 75.

NOTES TO THE WARES

39. The list is described in Bernard Rackham and H. J. Plenderleith, "The Material of the English Frit Porcelains," *Burlington Mag.*, LI (1927), 134–144. There would be no apparent reason for Bonnin and Morris to add bone ash to an avowedly earthenware body.

40. I am much indebted to Hugh Tait and A. E. Werner for their kind offer and to Calvin Hathaway for his cooperation. On the basis of three spot tests and this author's judgment that the Bonnin and Morris wares were soft-paste porcelain, Marvin D. Schwartz and Richard Wolfe in *A History of American Art Porcelain* (New York, 1967), 16–17 (previewed in *Antiques*, XCI [1967], 154), without any appropriate recognition, "reclassified" the Bonnin and Morris pieces as porcelain; the account of the factory contained therein is almost wholly inaccurate.

41. A fragment from the site of the factory with this border is illustrated in W. W. R. Spelman, *Lowestoft China* (London, 1905), pl. LII, upper row, third from left.

42. "P" was occasionally used as a mark on early Worcester, but there is little similarity between these products and the two fruit baskets in question. An un-

painted Lowestoft figure similar to that in the Watney Collection is shown in the catalogue of the *Antique Porcelain Company* (June 1951), pl. 23; painted Lowestoft figures in the Victoria and Albert Museum differ in this detail.

43. A Lowestoft basket is shown in Watney, *English Blue and White Porcelain*, pl. 73B.

44. *Ibid.*, pp. 64–65, pls. 53, 55.

45. *Ibid.*, pl. 55B.

46. *Ibid.*, pls. 16C and 65A.

47. *Ibid.*, pl. 73C.

48. *Ibid.*, pls. 13B and 13C.

49. *Ibid.*, pl. 17C.

50. I am very grateful to the General Motors Research Laboratory, in particular to Miss Alberta Harrington, Dr. Nils Muench, and Mr. Albert Ottolini, for the microprobe spectrographic analysis of this waster. The analysis revealed that the red decoration lay beneath the lead glaze and consisted largely of iron.

Index

———————◆•◆———————

[77]

A Note on the Book

———◆•◆———

Text set in Granjon Linotype

Display lines set in Caslon Foundry

Text composition and printing by Heritage Printers, Inc.,
Charlotte, North Carolina, on
Sixty-pound Glatfelter Old Forge Laid FF White B-52 paper by
P. H. Glatfelter Co., Spring Grove, Pennsylvania

Illustration insert printed by Washburn Press,
Charlotte, North Carolina, on
Seventy-pound Cameo Dull Enamel paper by
S. D. Warren Co., Boston, Massachusetts

Binding by Kingsport Press, Inc.,
Kingsport, Tennessee

Designed and published by
The University of North Carolina Press,
Chapel Hill, North Carolina